In this artistic haven, we invite you on a spiritual and creative journey, where inner peace intertwines with celestial beauty.

Each page of this book is an invitation to explore the symbolism of angels and archangels, delving into the depths of their benevolent energies.

By coloring each mandala, you not only express your creativity but also connect with the sacred.

Let yourself be enveloped by the delicate lines that outline angelic figures, and allow the chosen colors to reflect the emotions and intentions that dwell in your heart and let your creations become a unique expression of your connection with the divine.

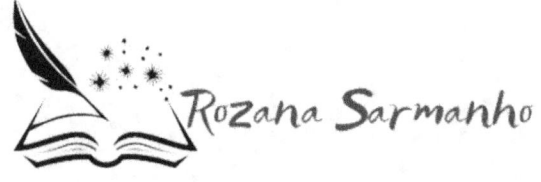

Rozana Sarmanho

Test Color Page

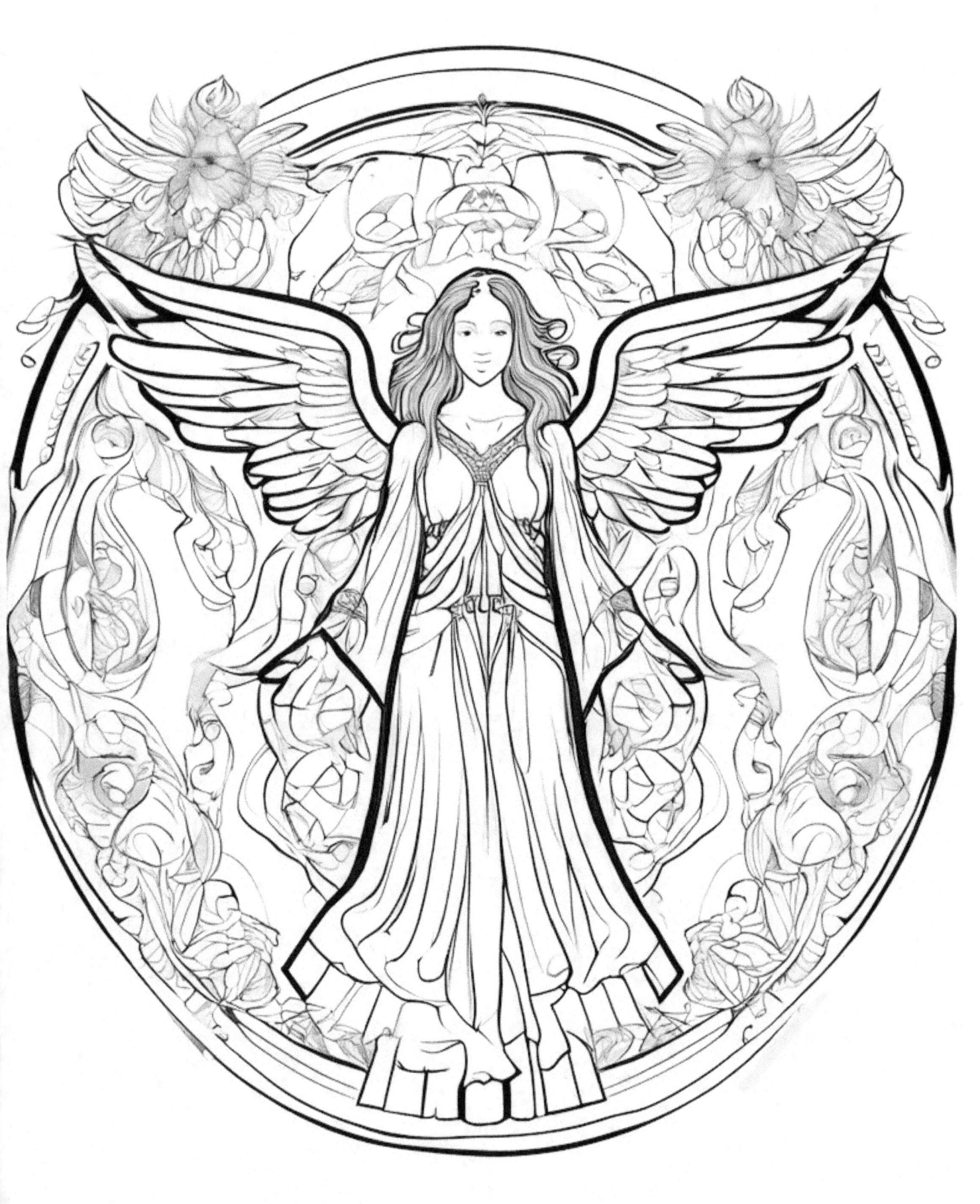

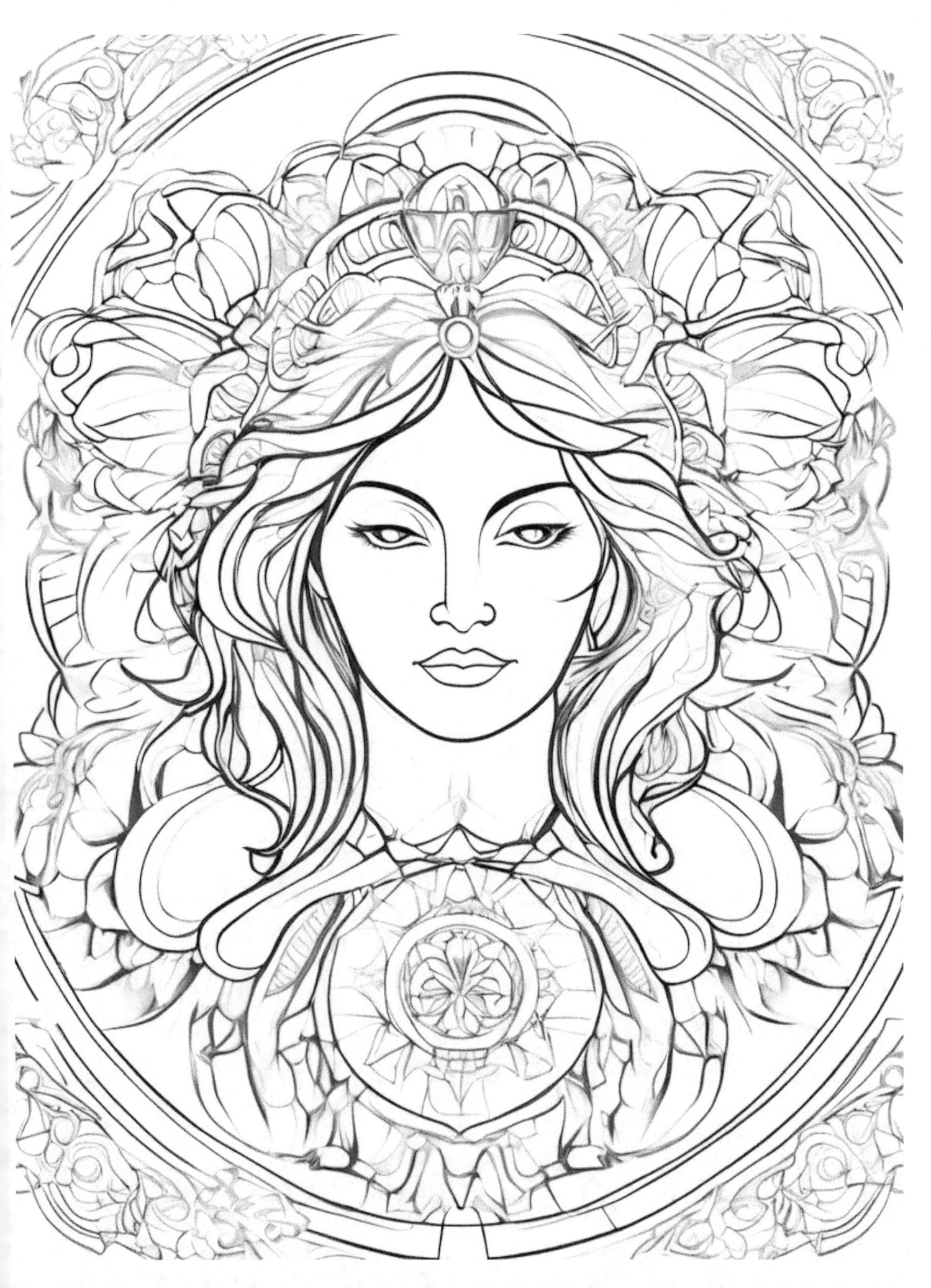

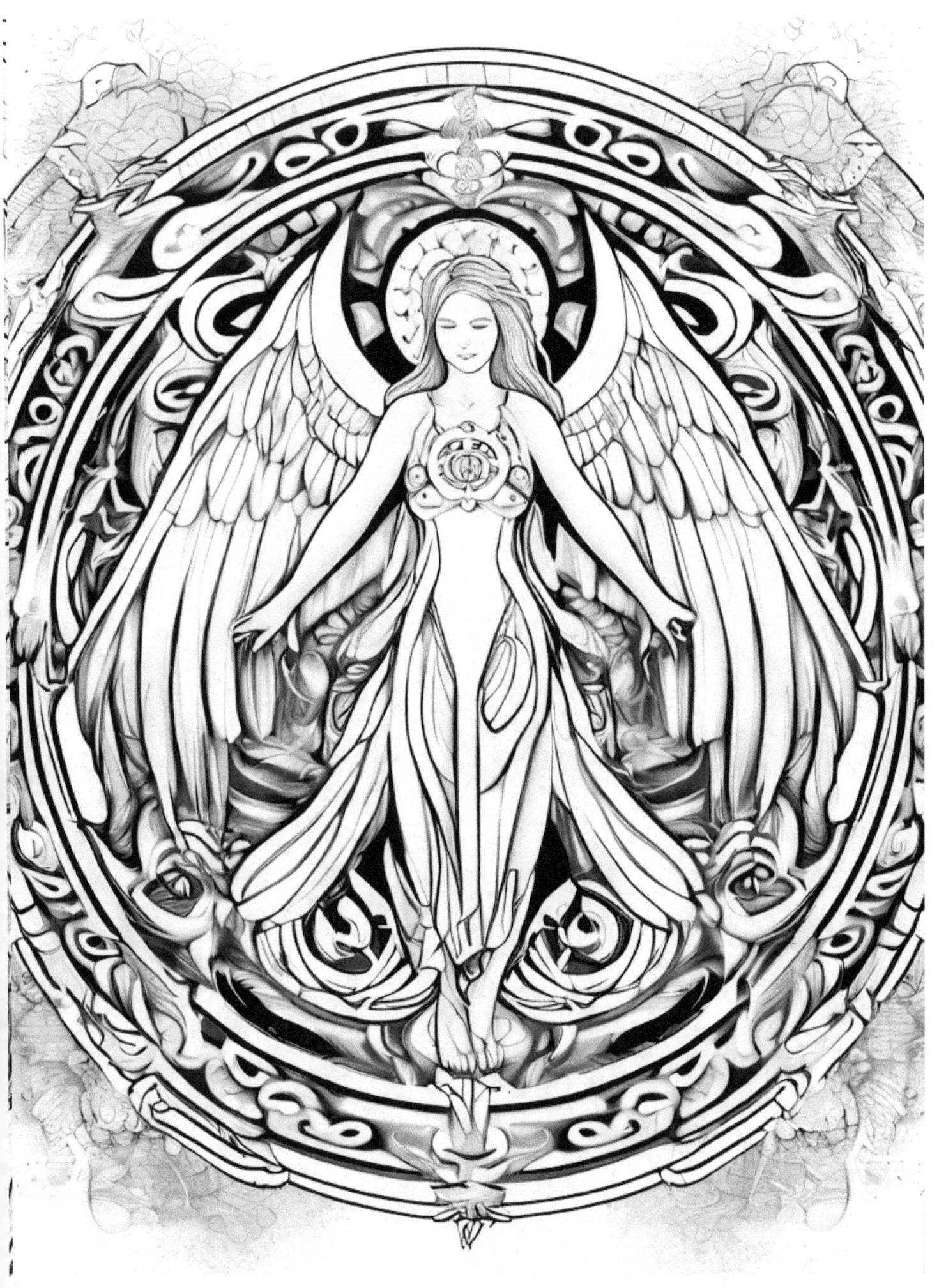

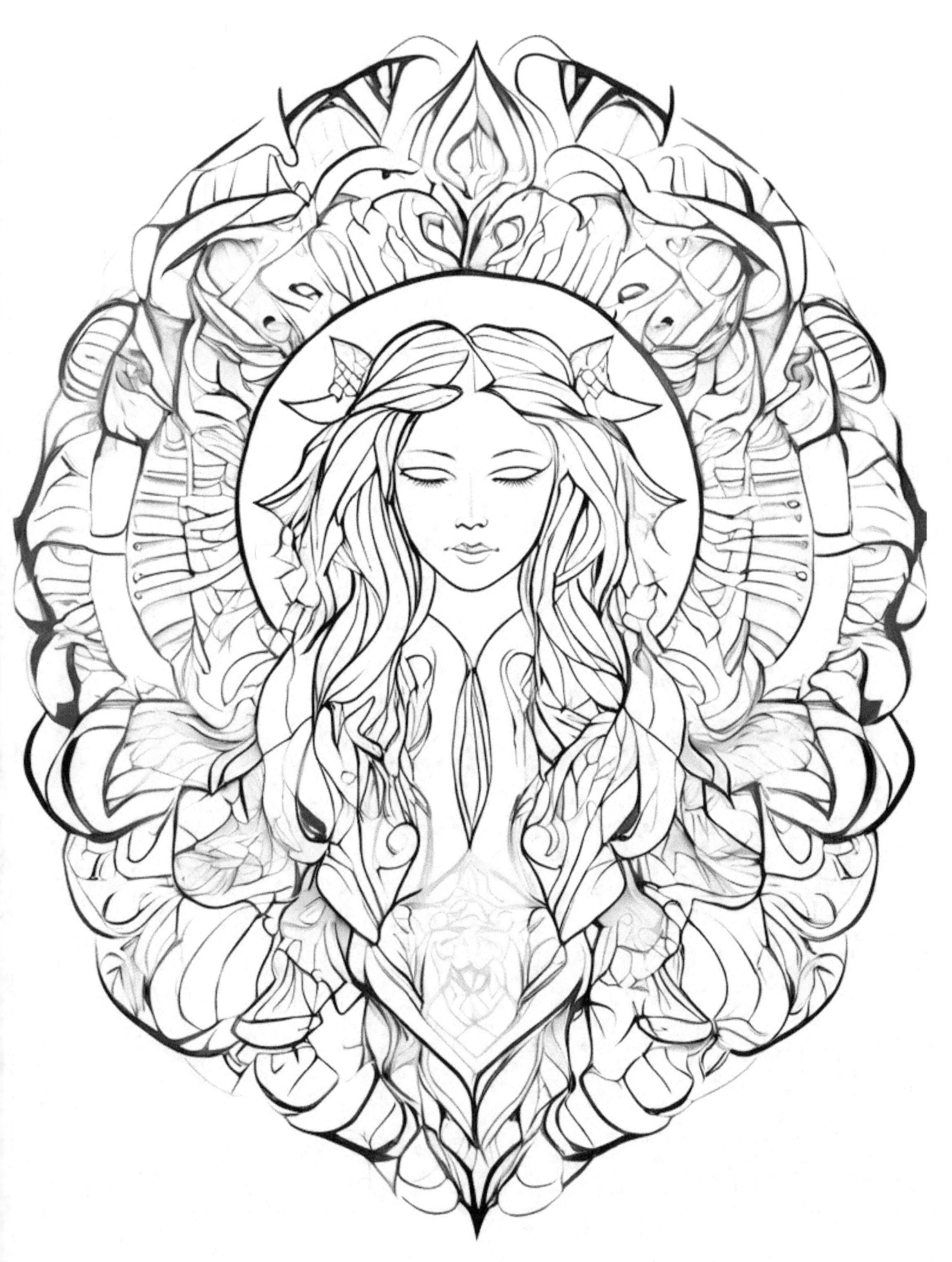

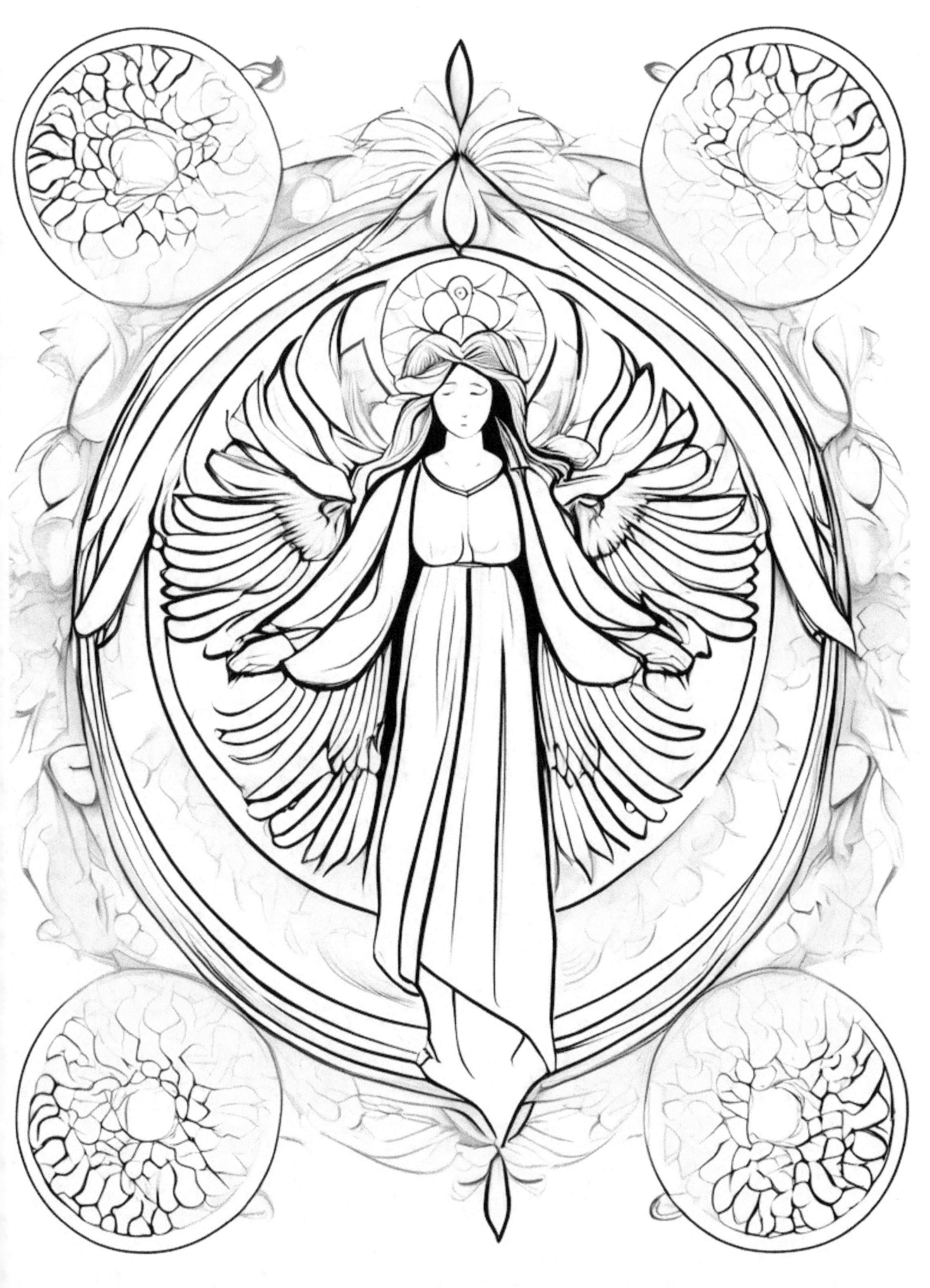

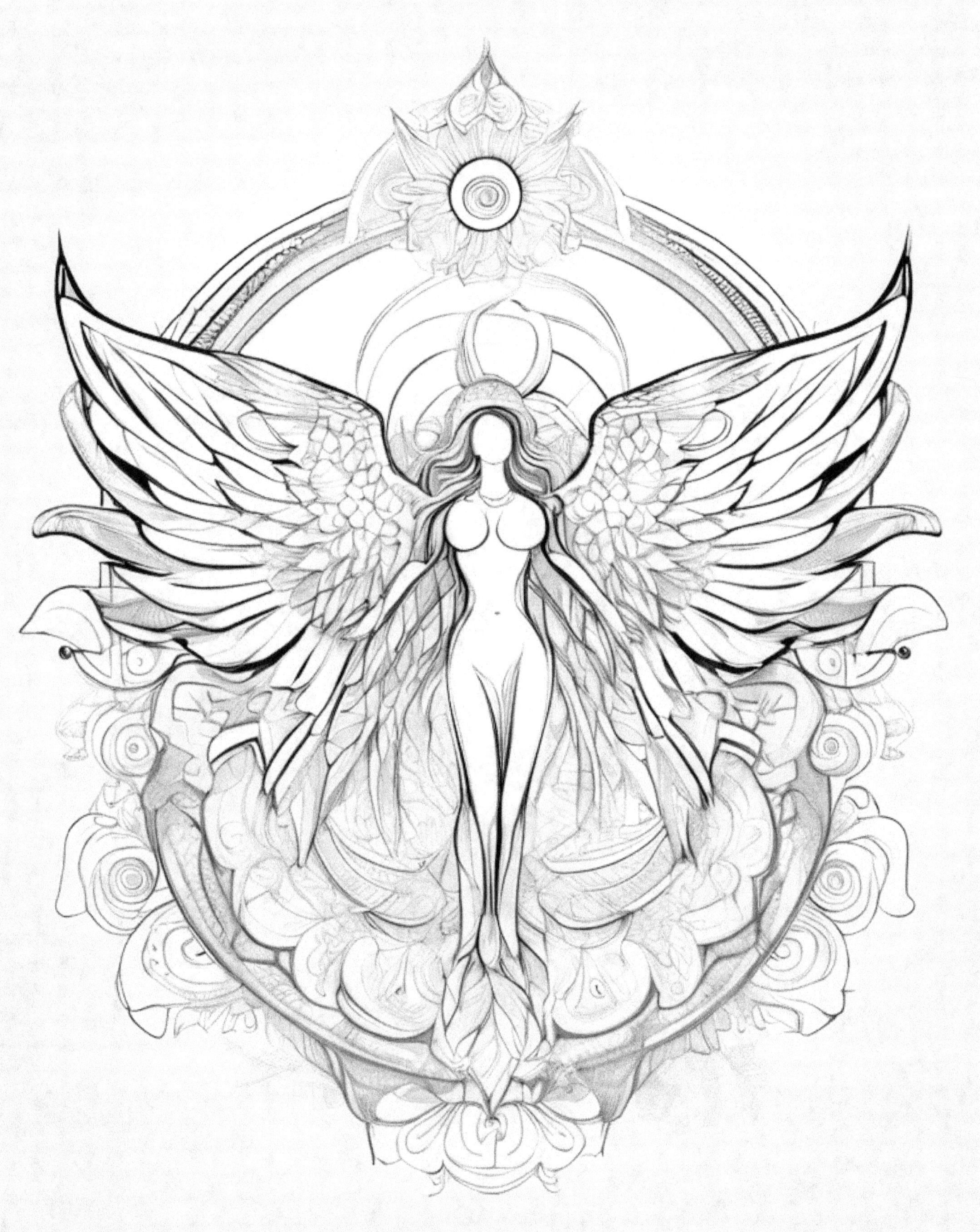

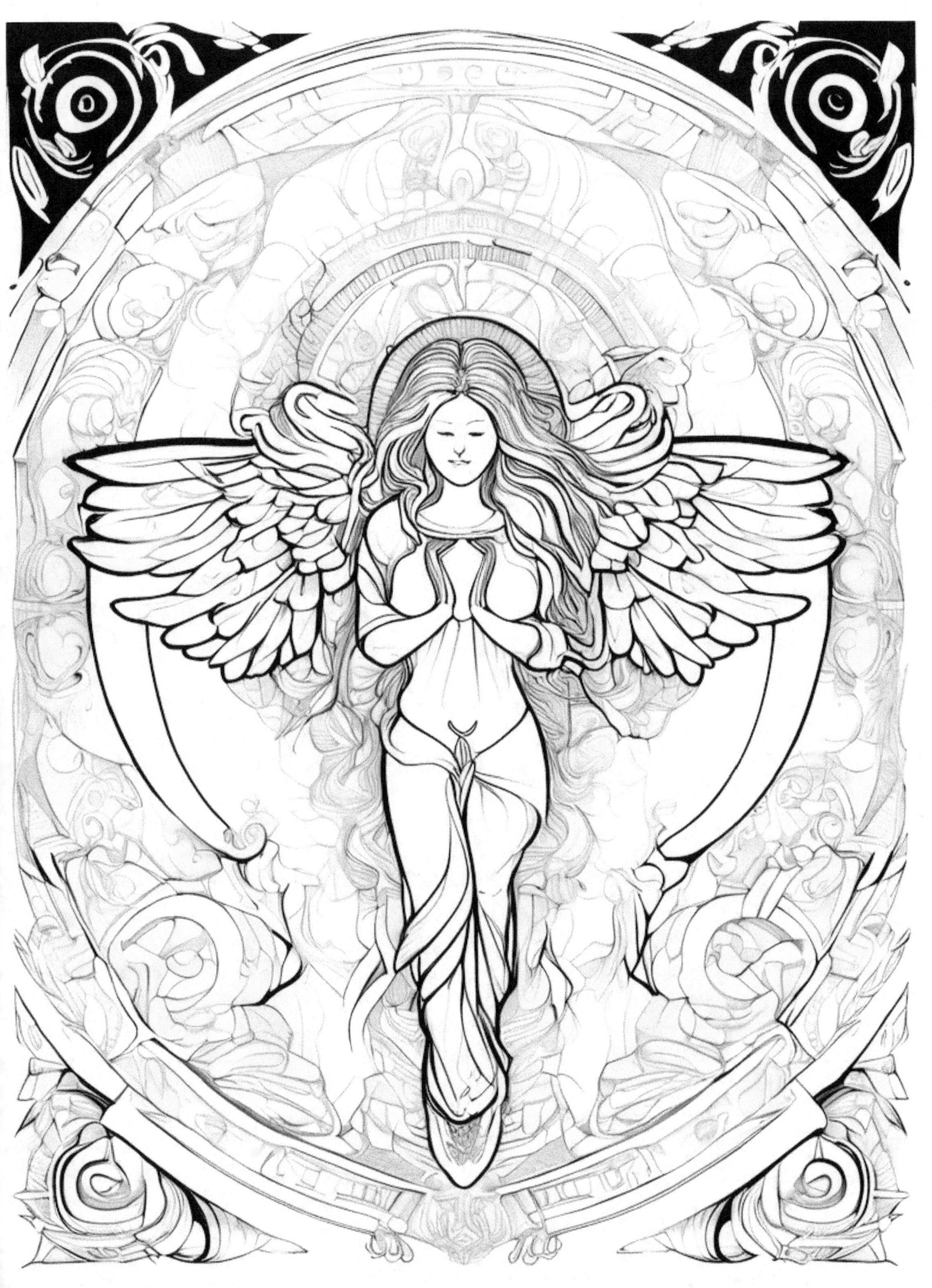

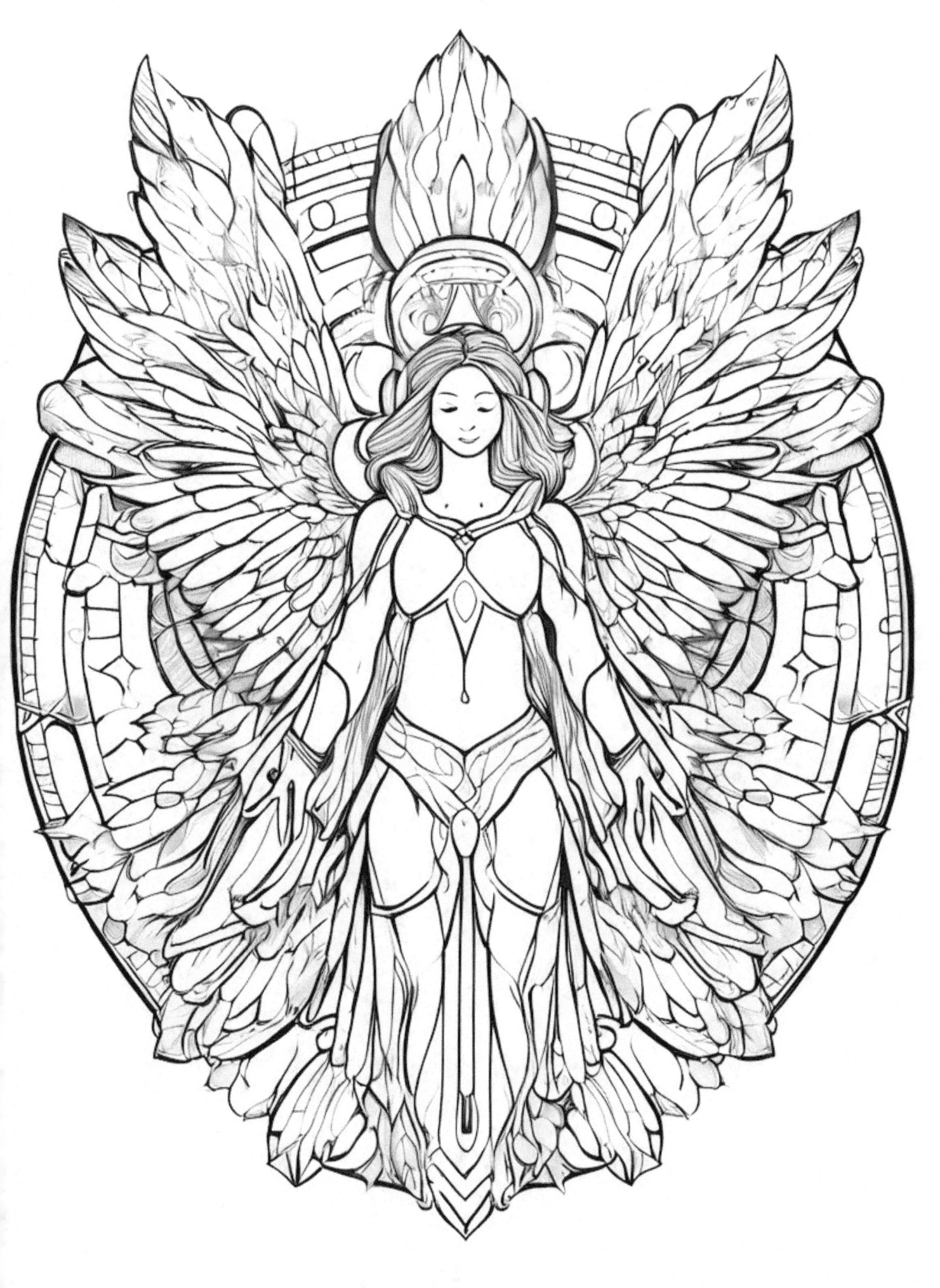

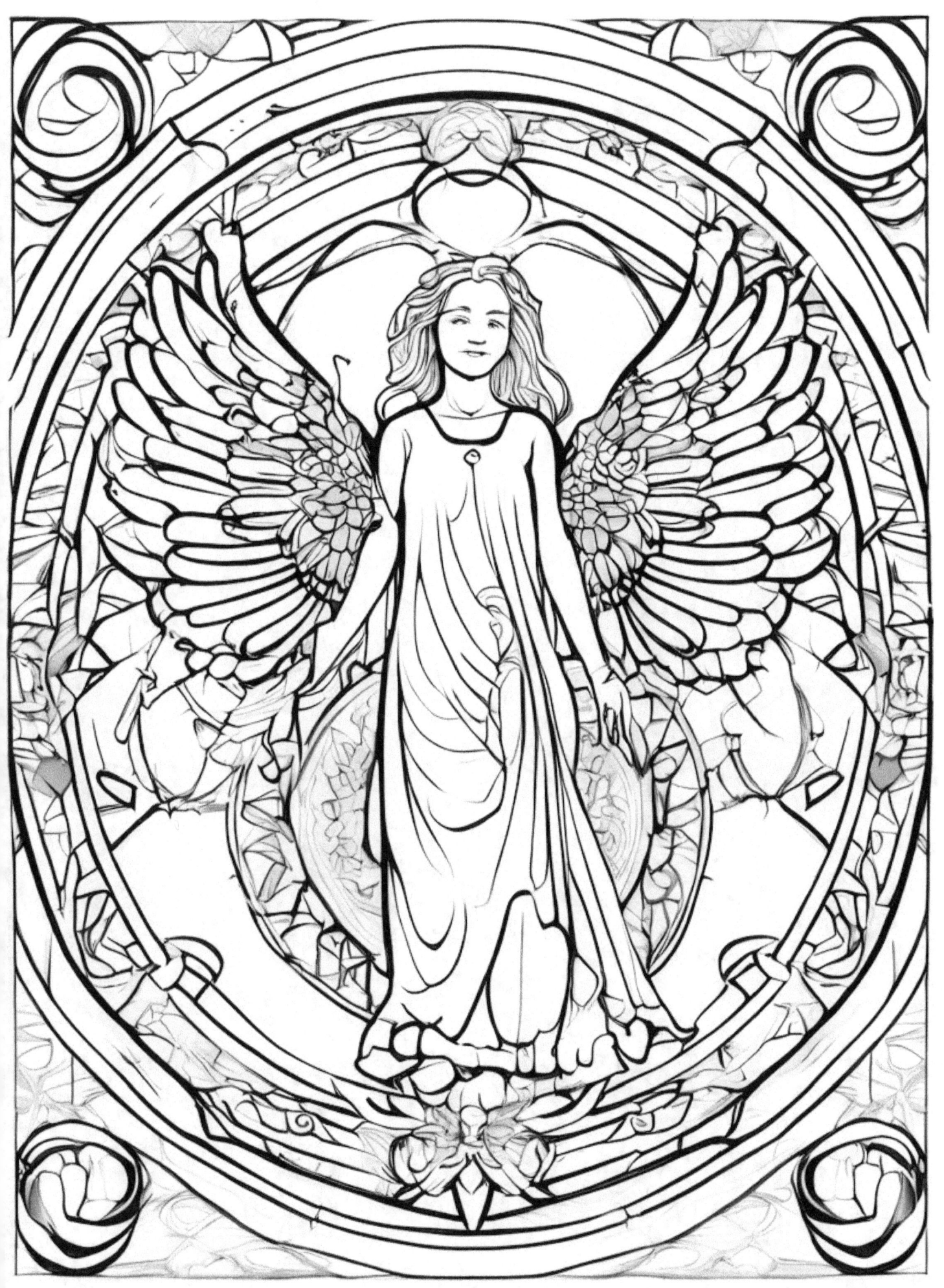

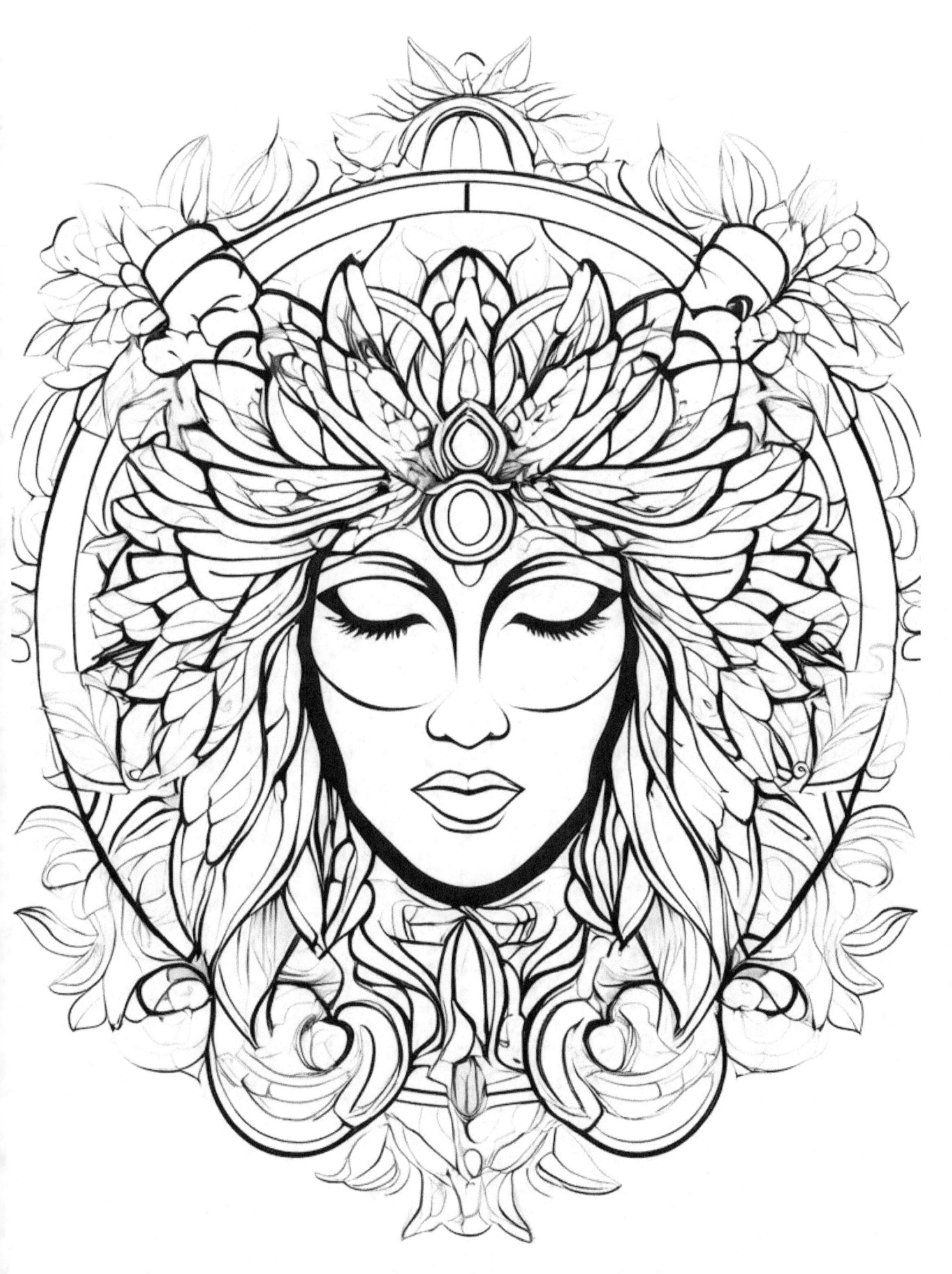

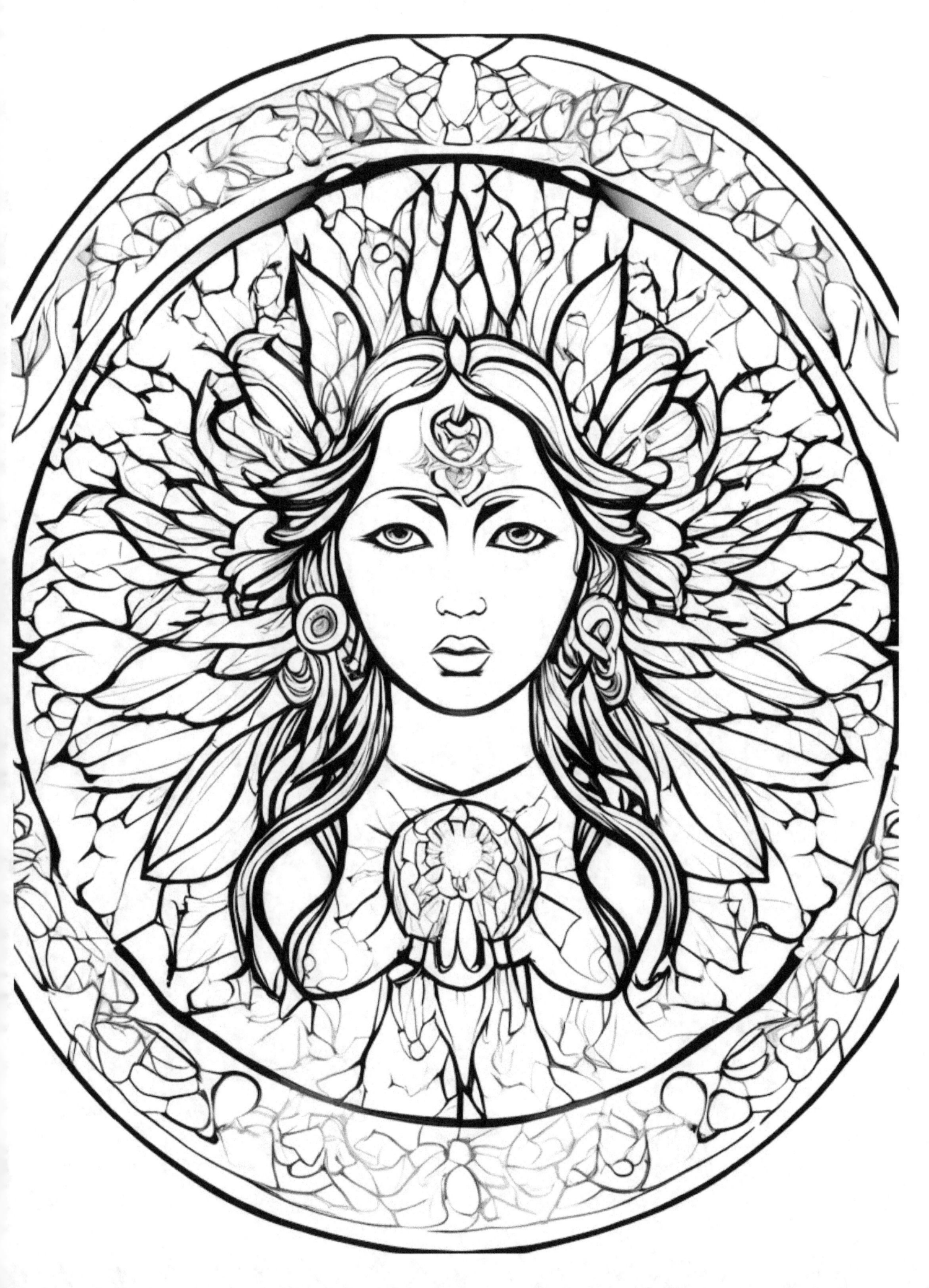

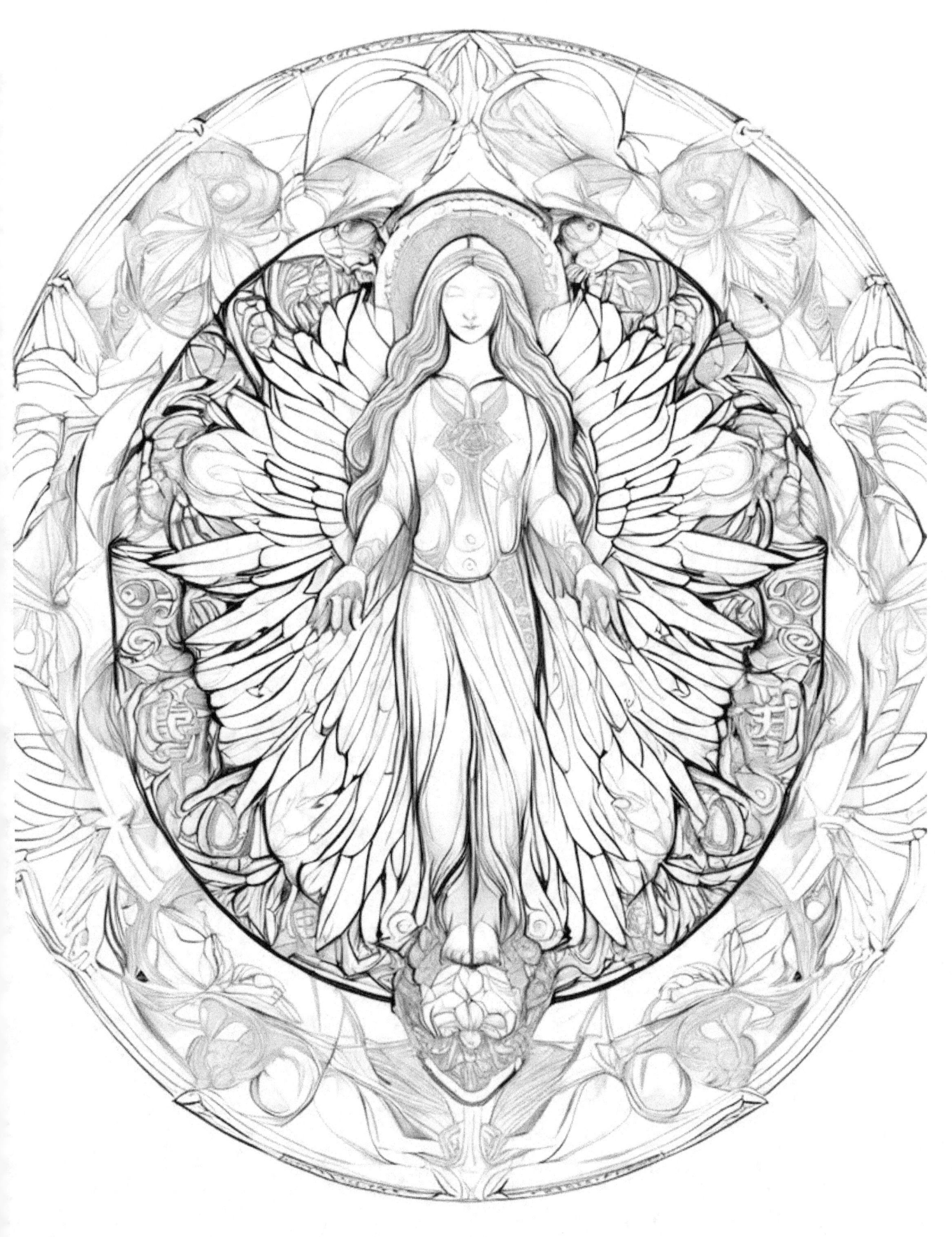

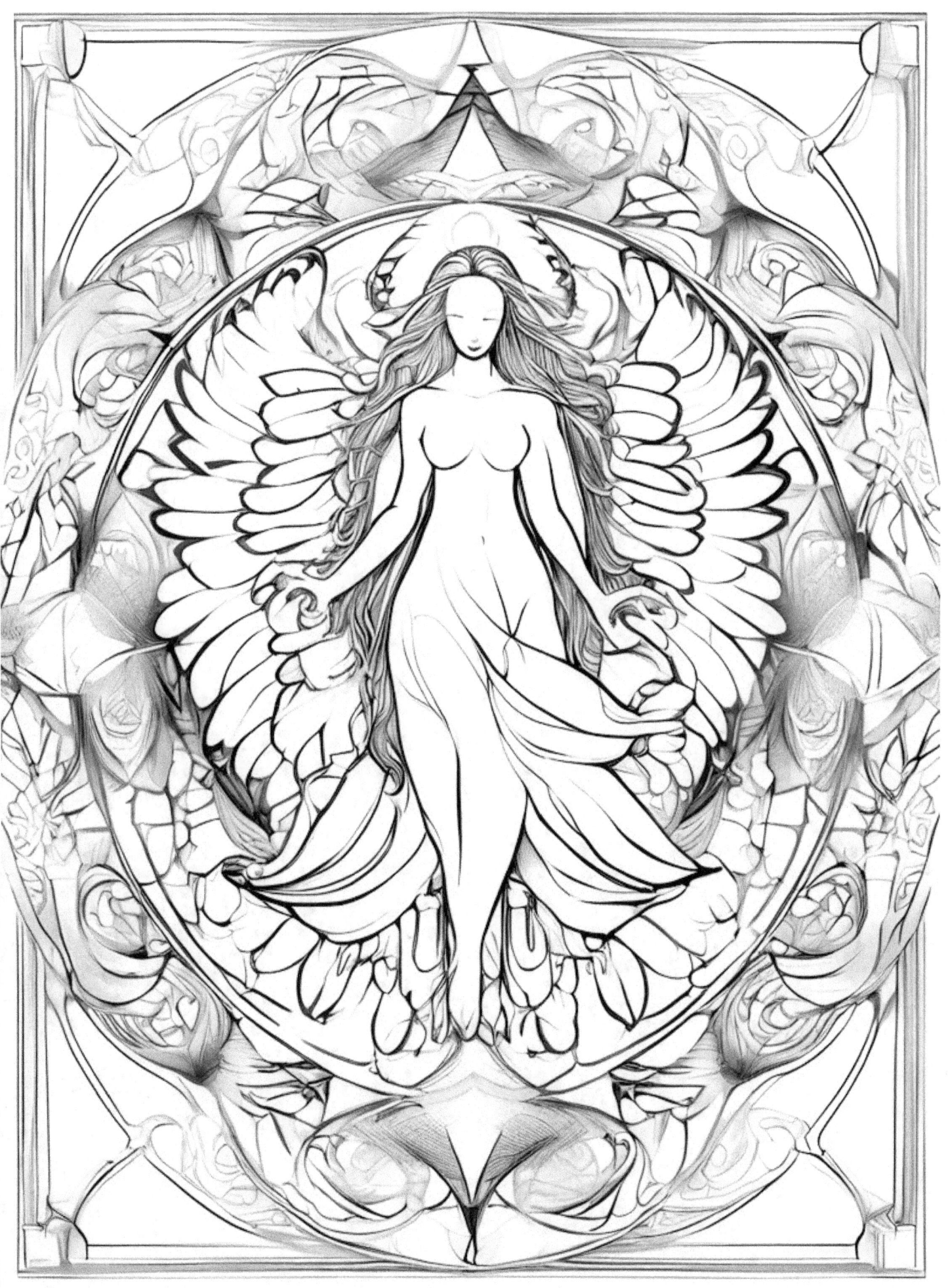

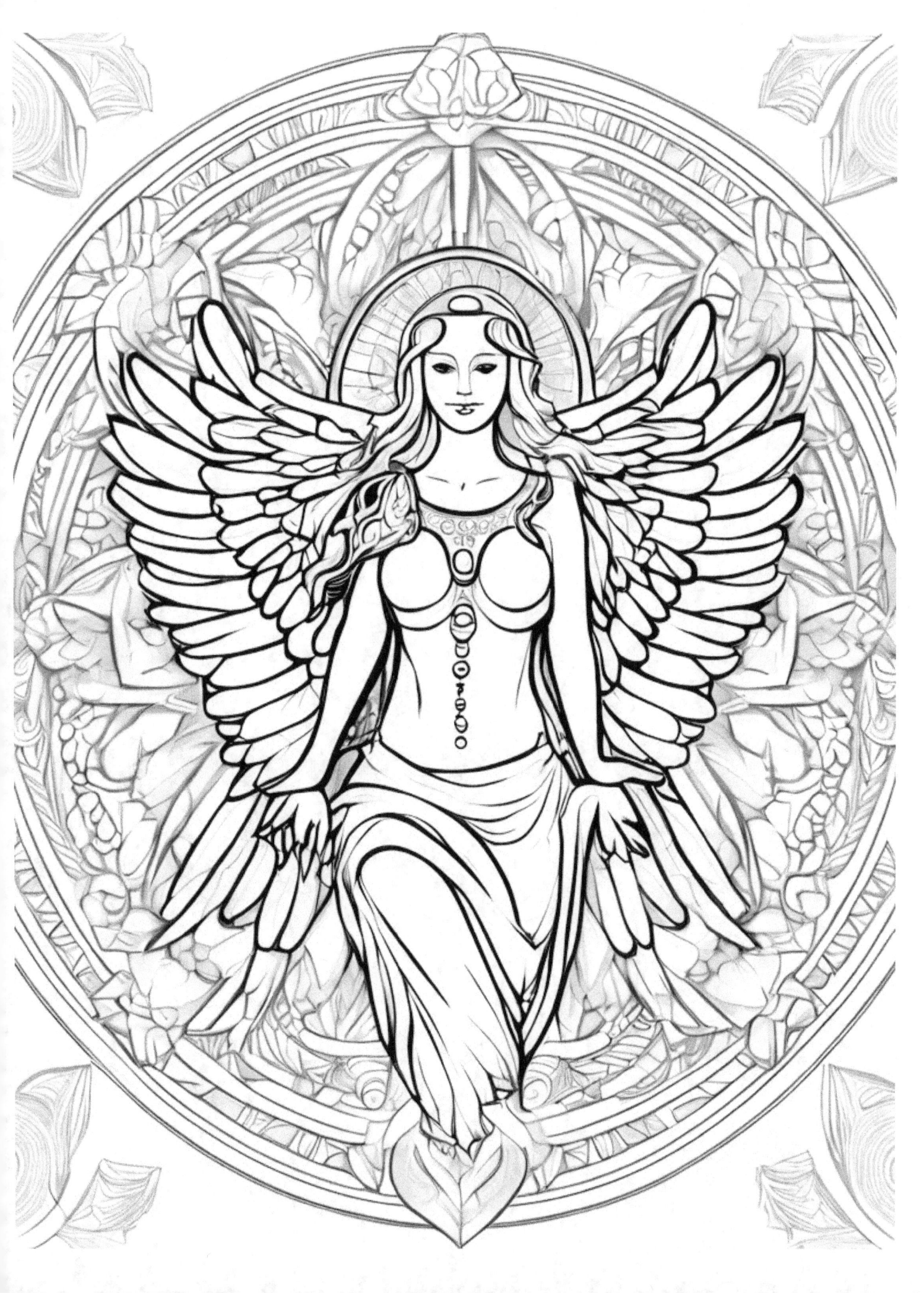

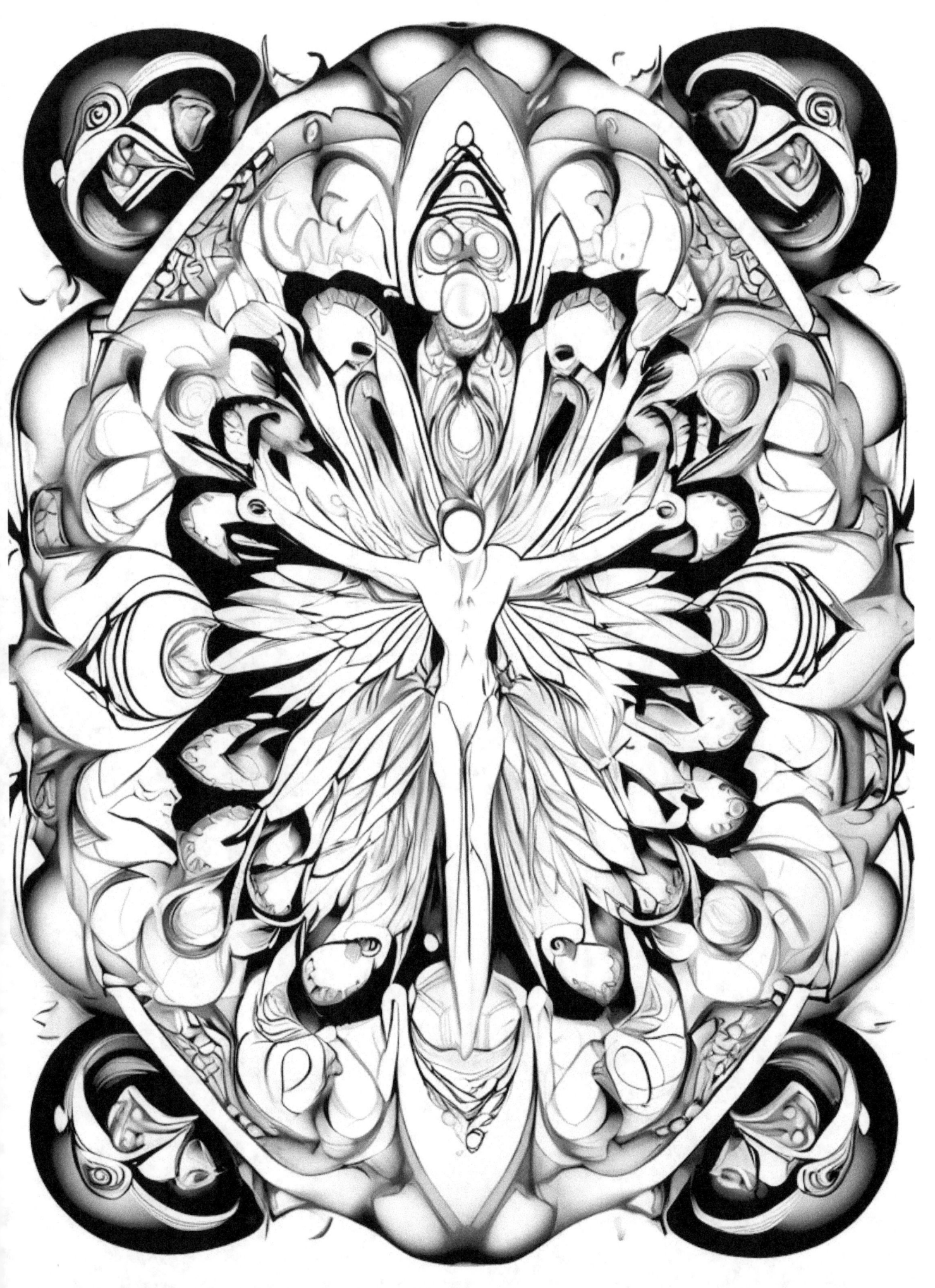

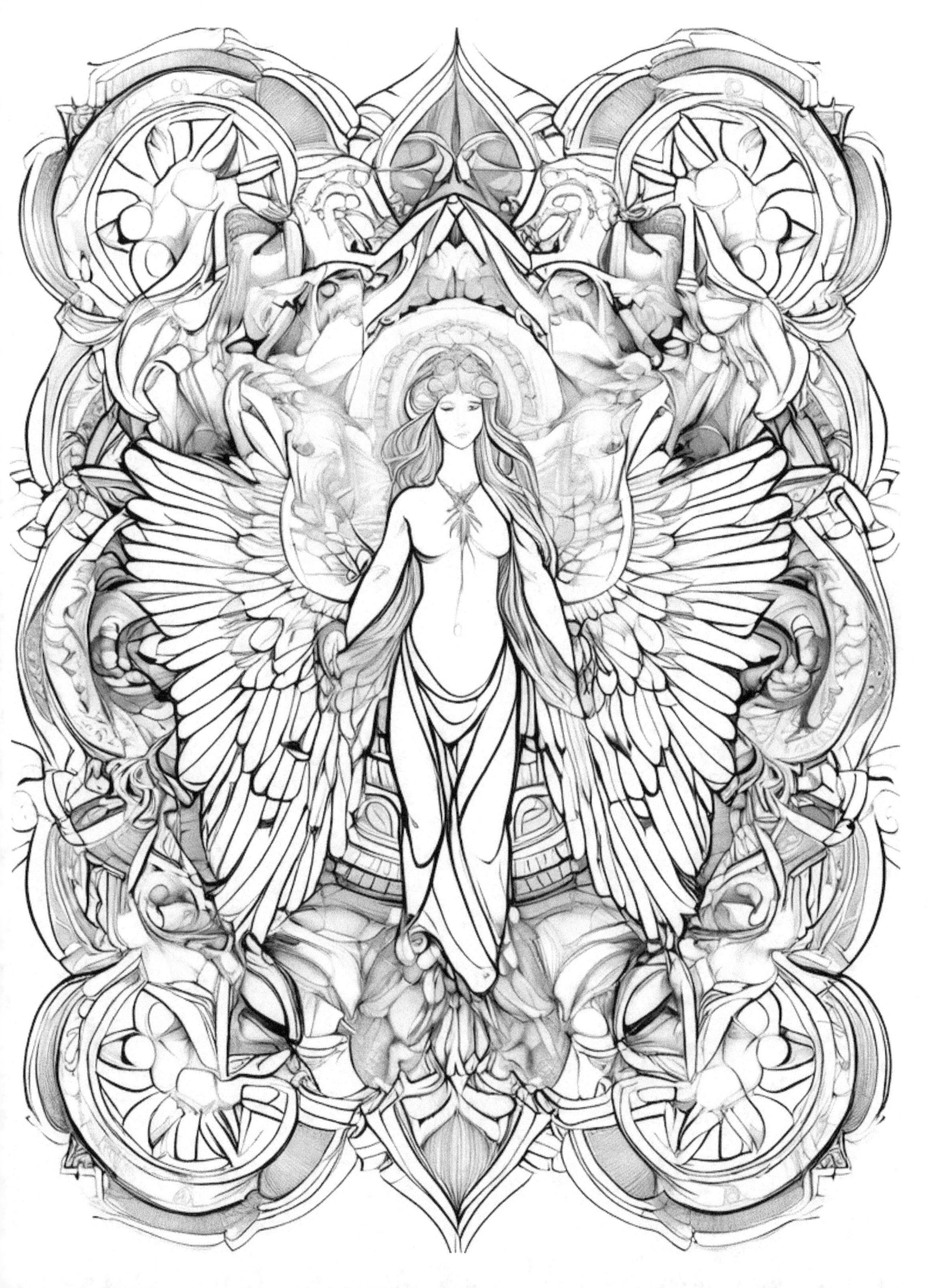

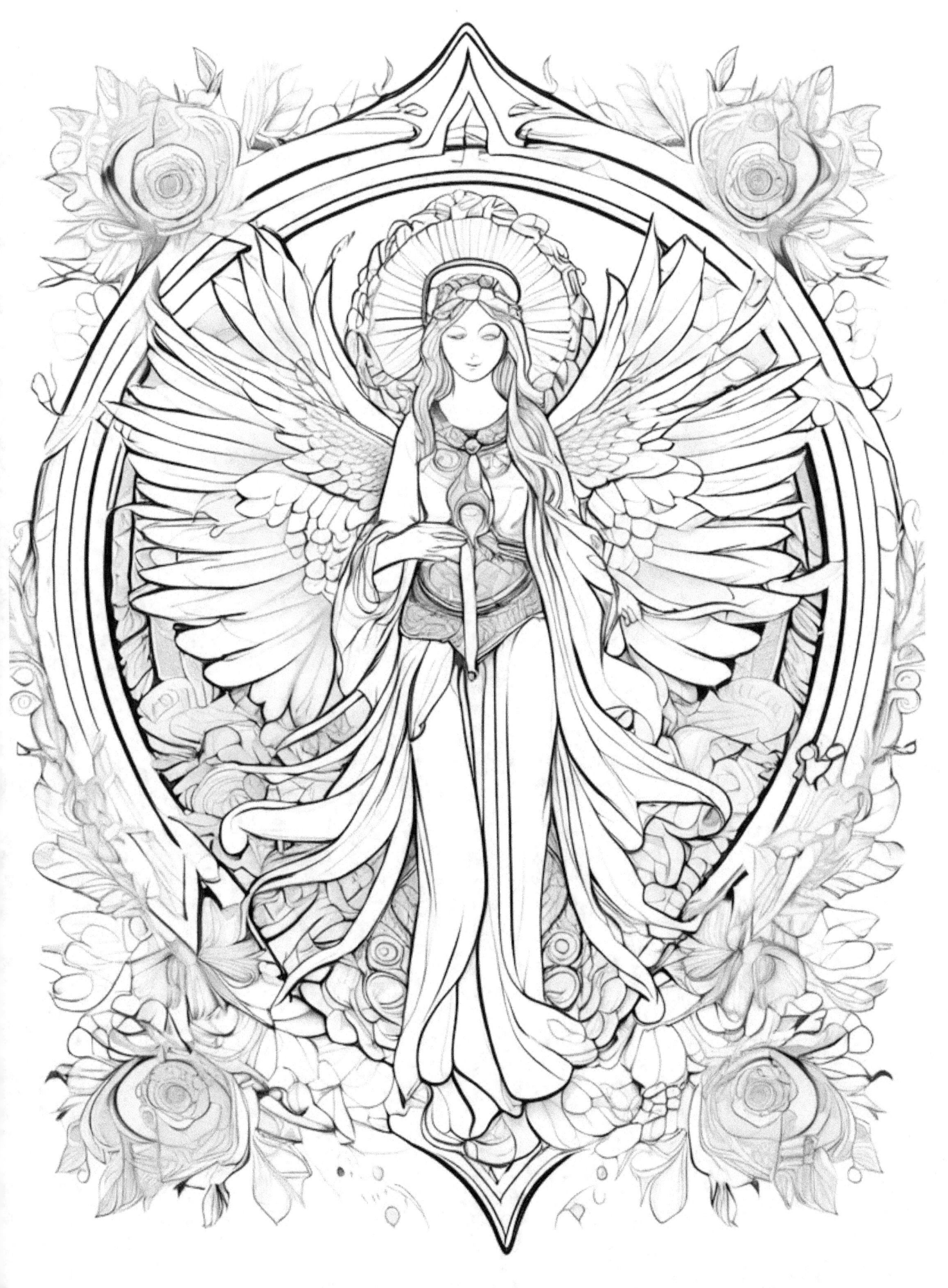

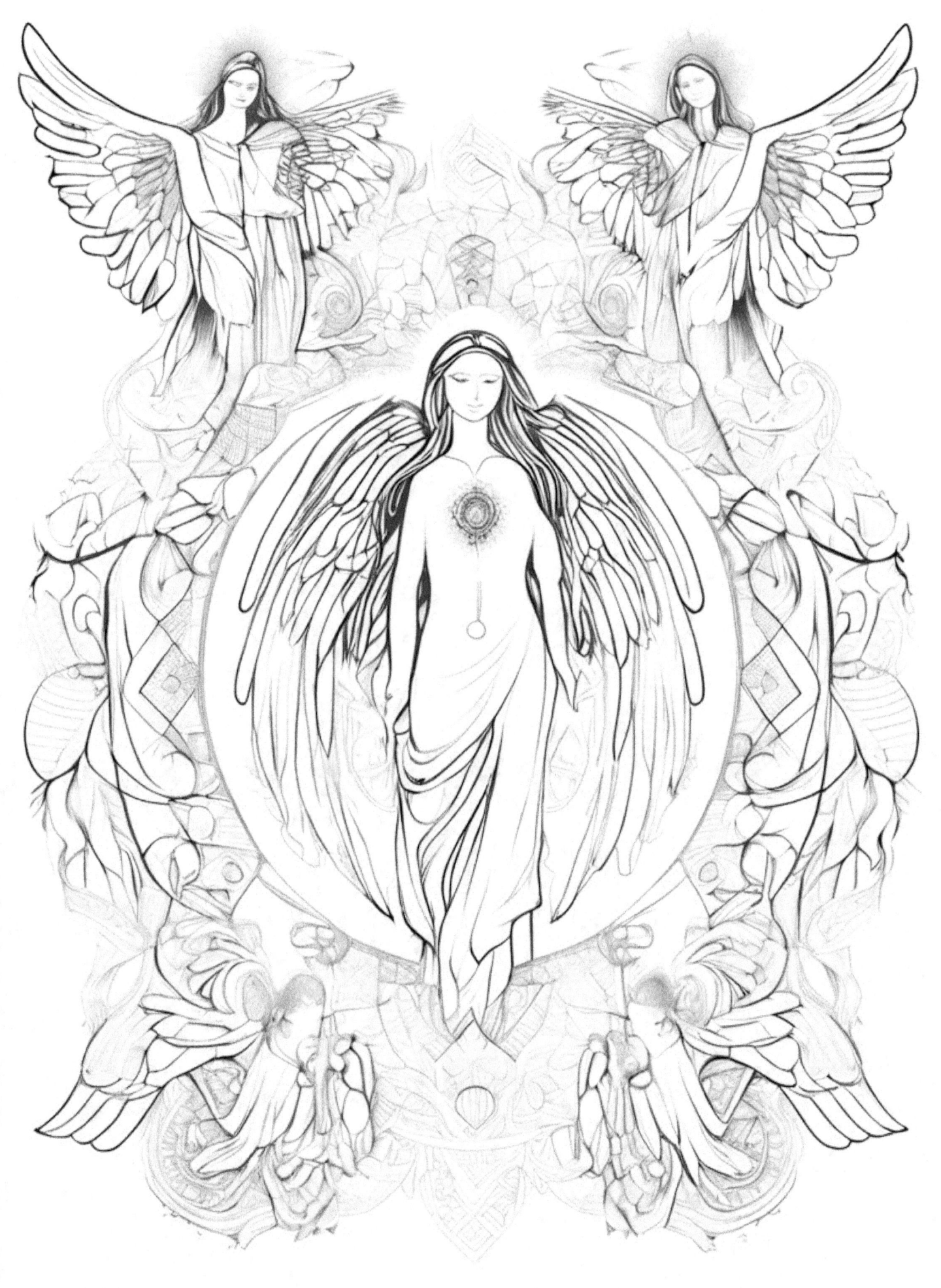

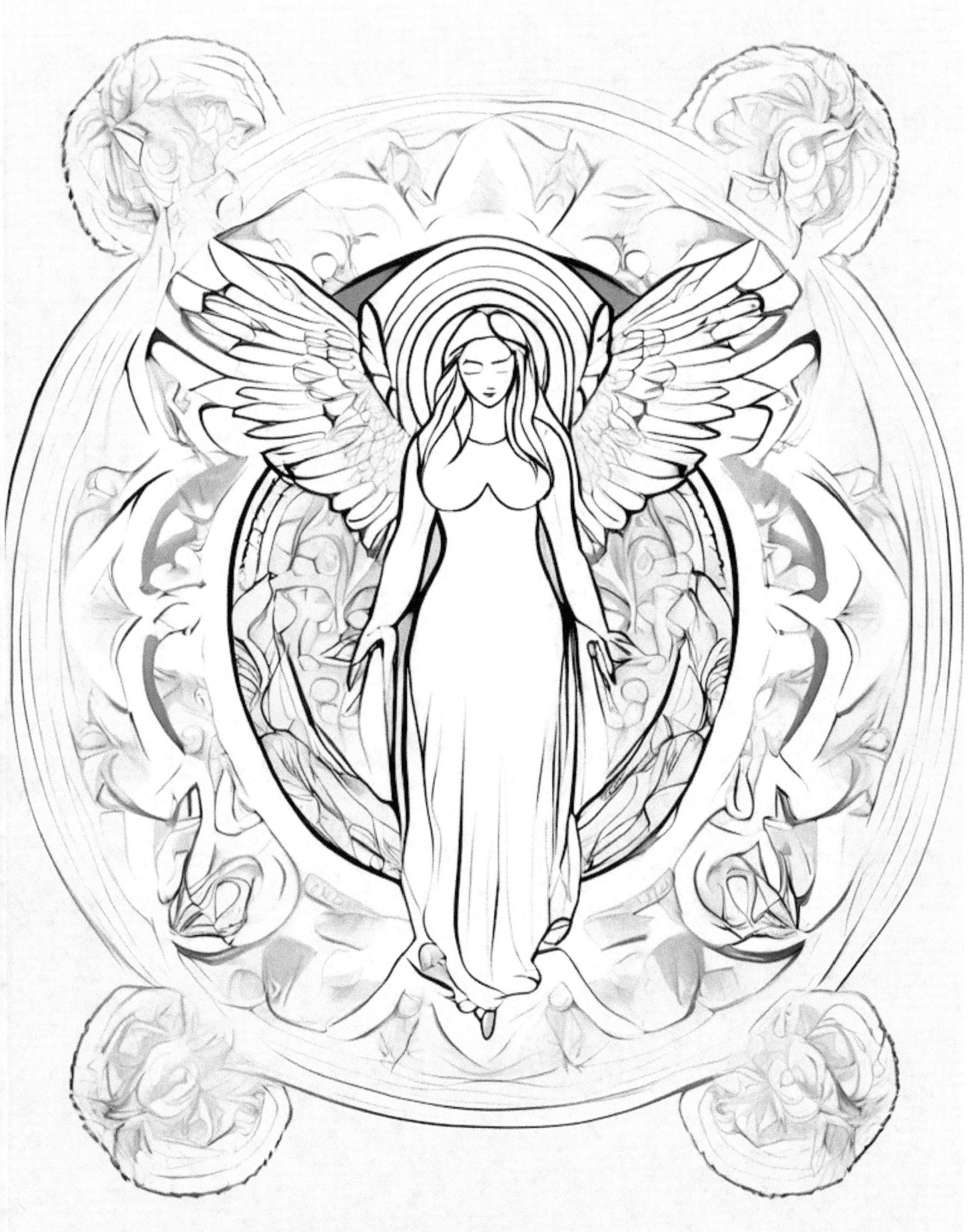

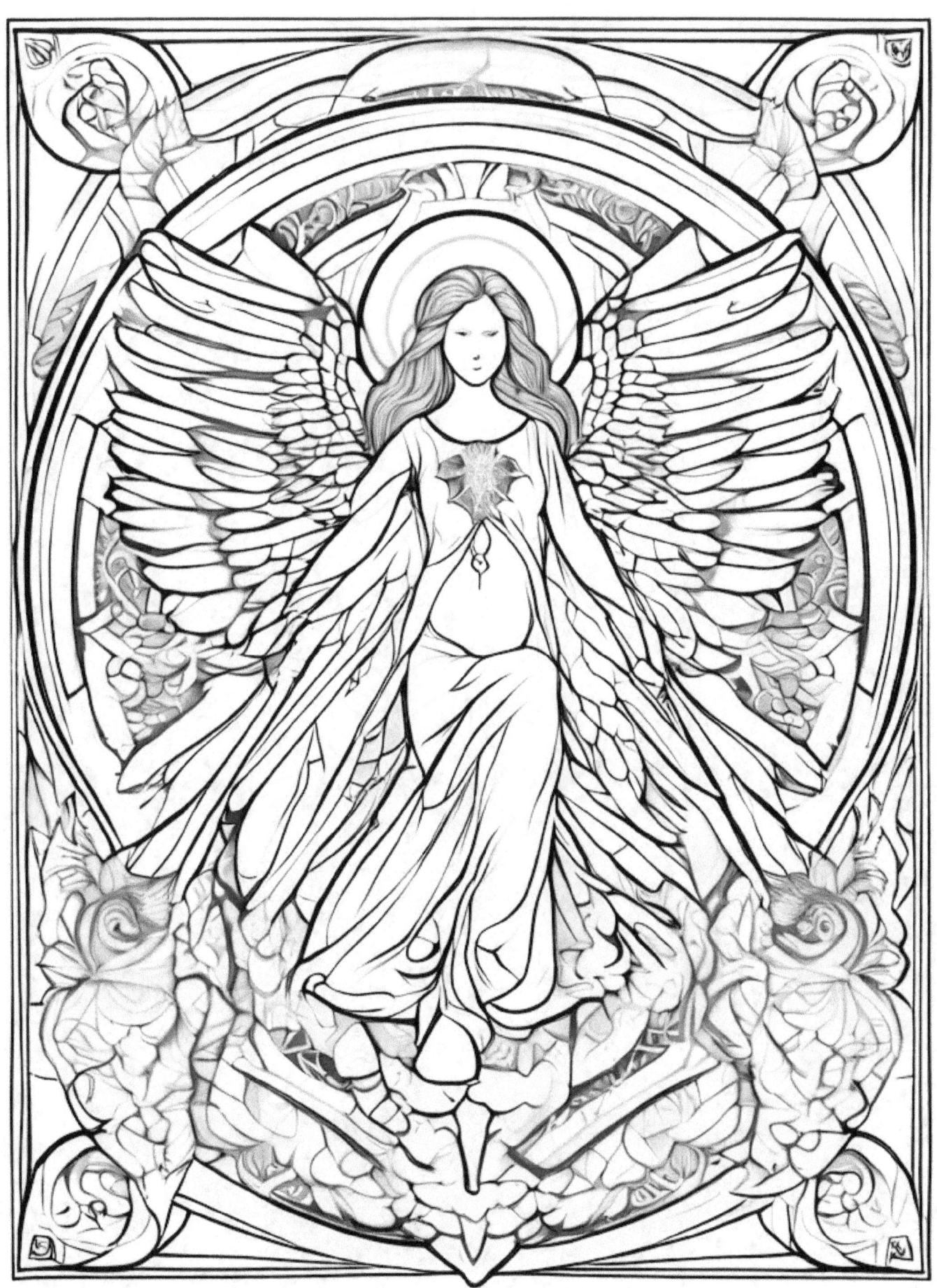

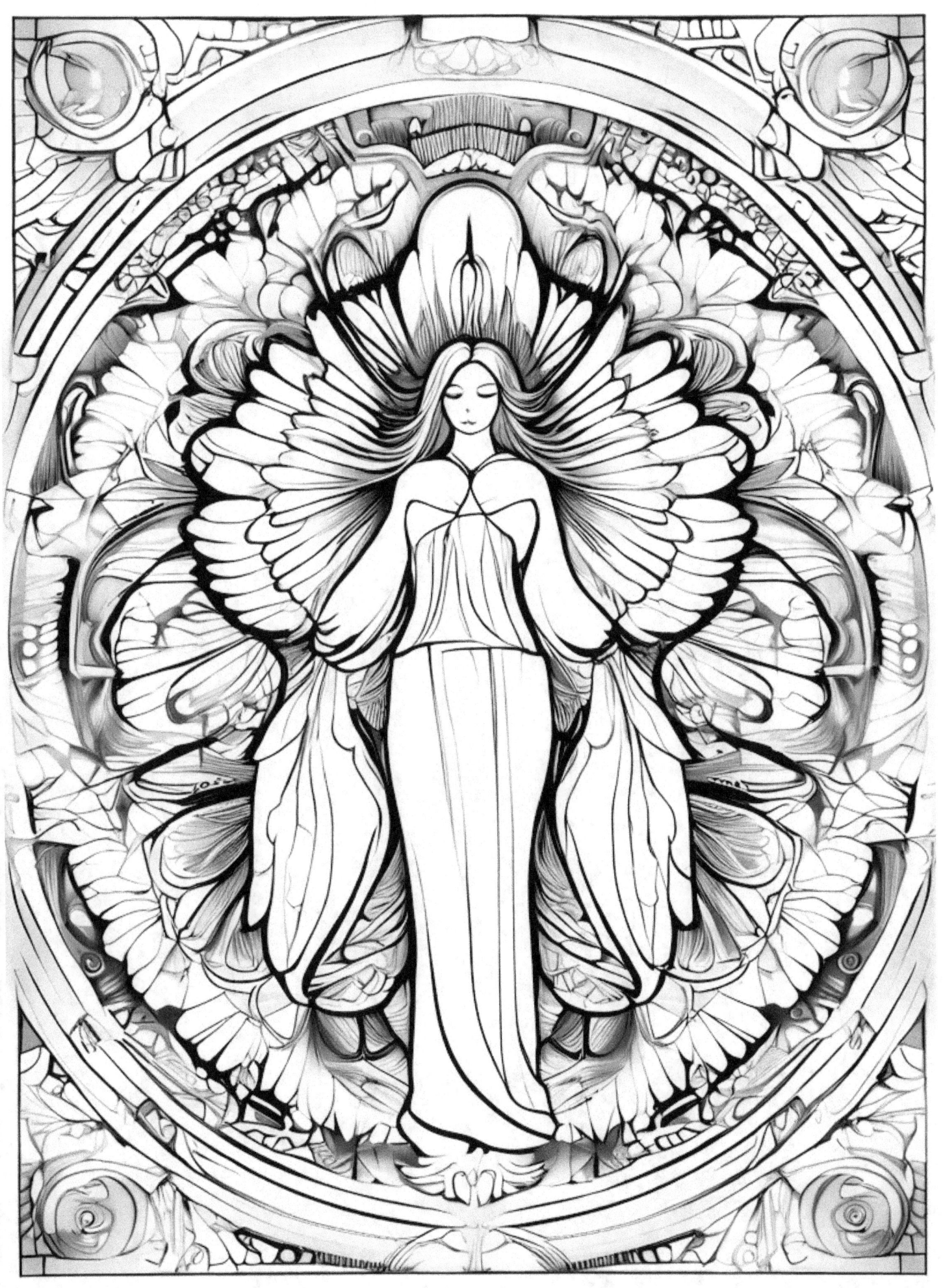

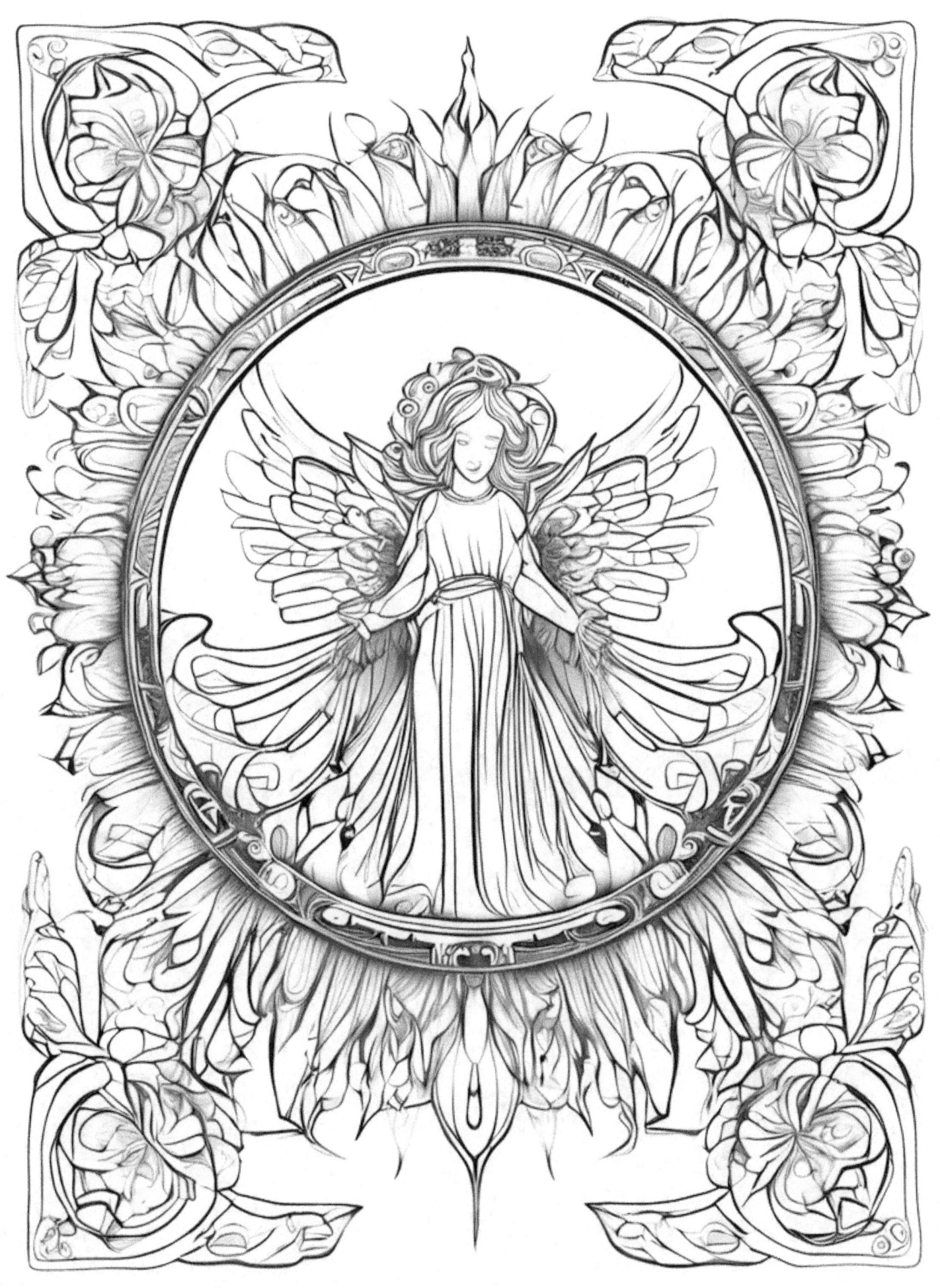

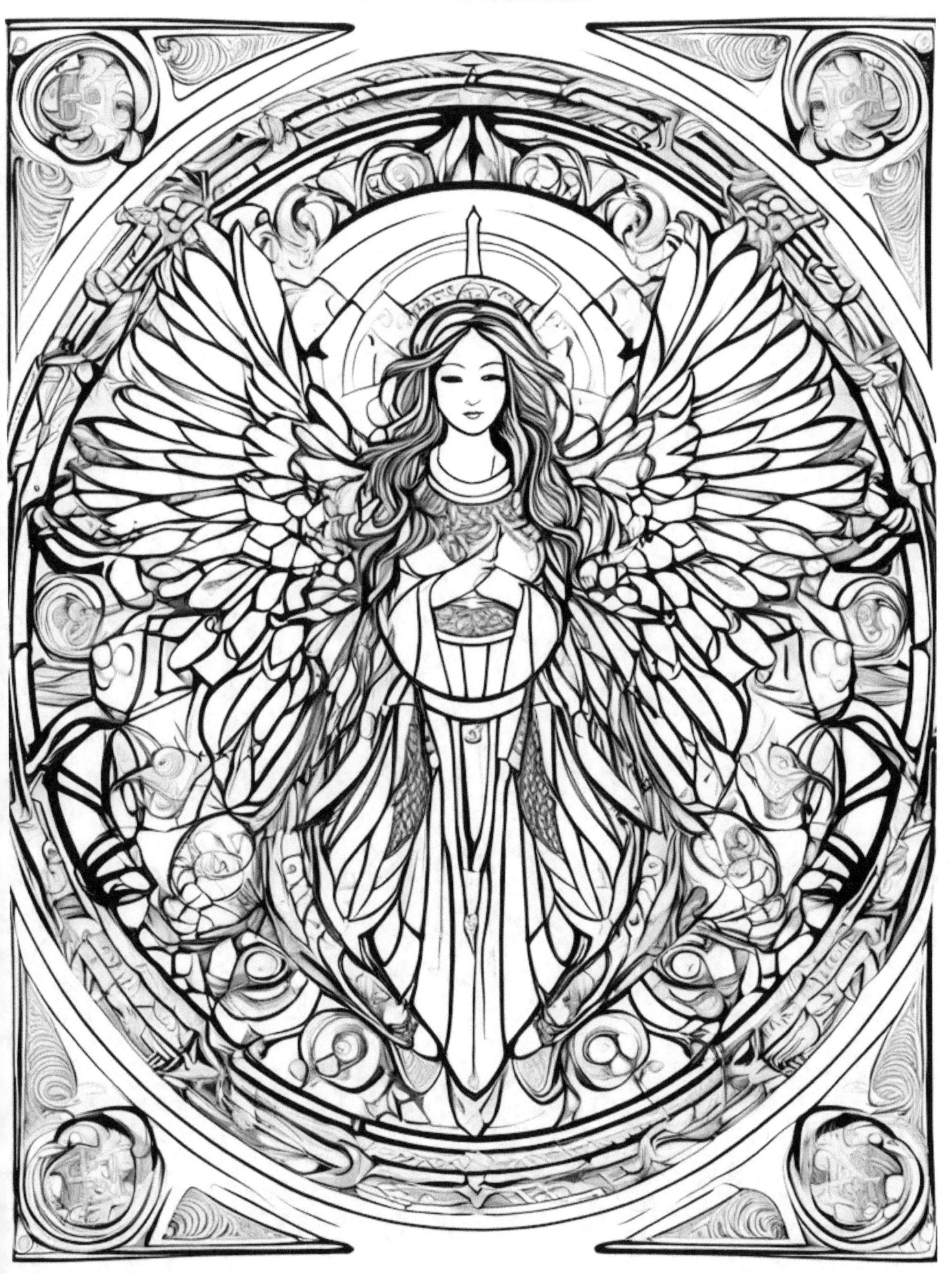

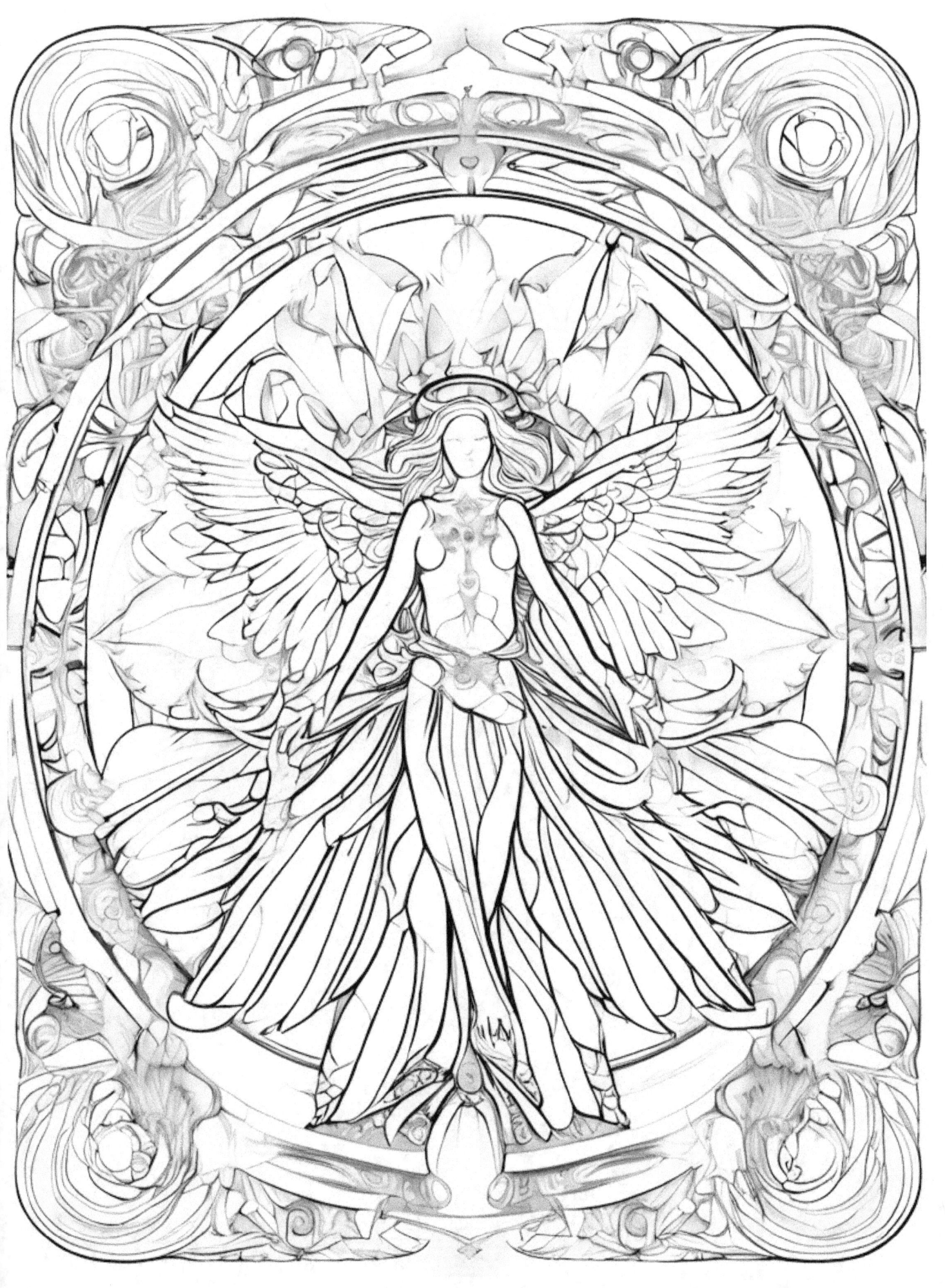

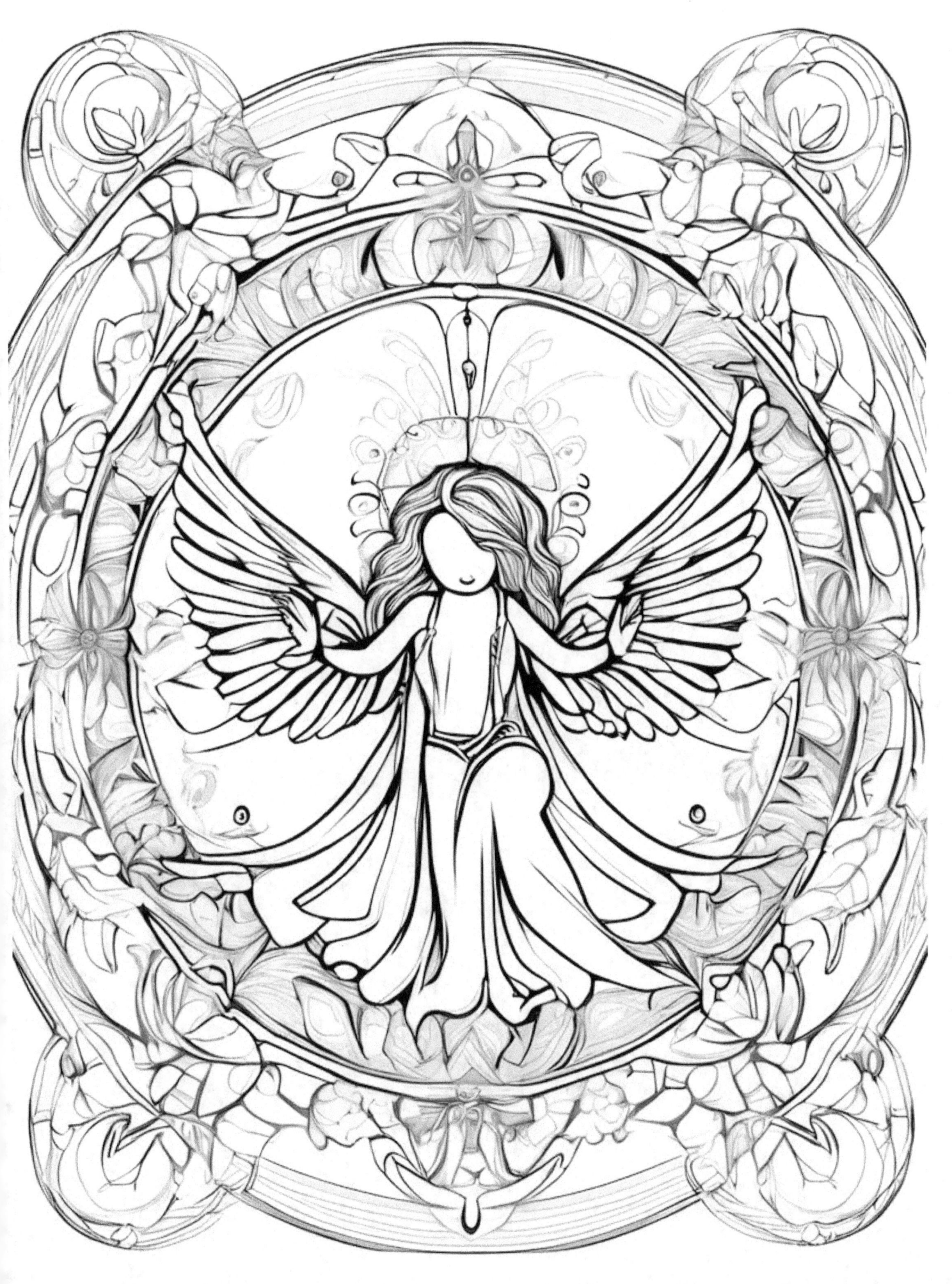

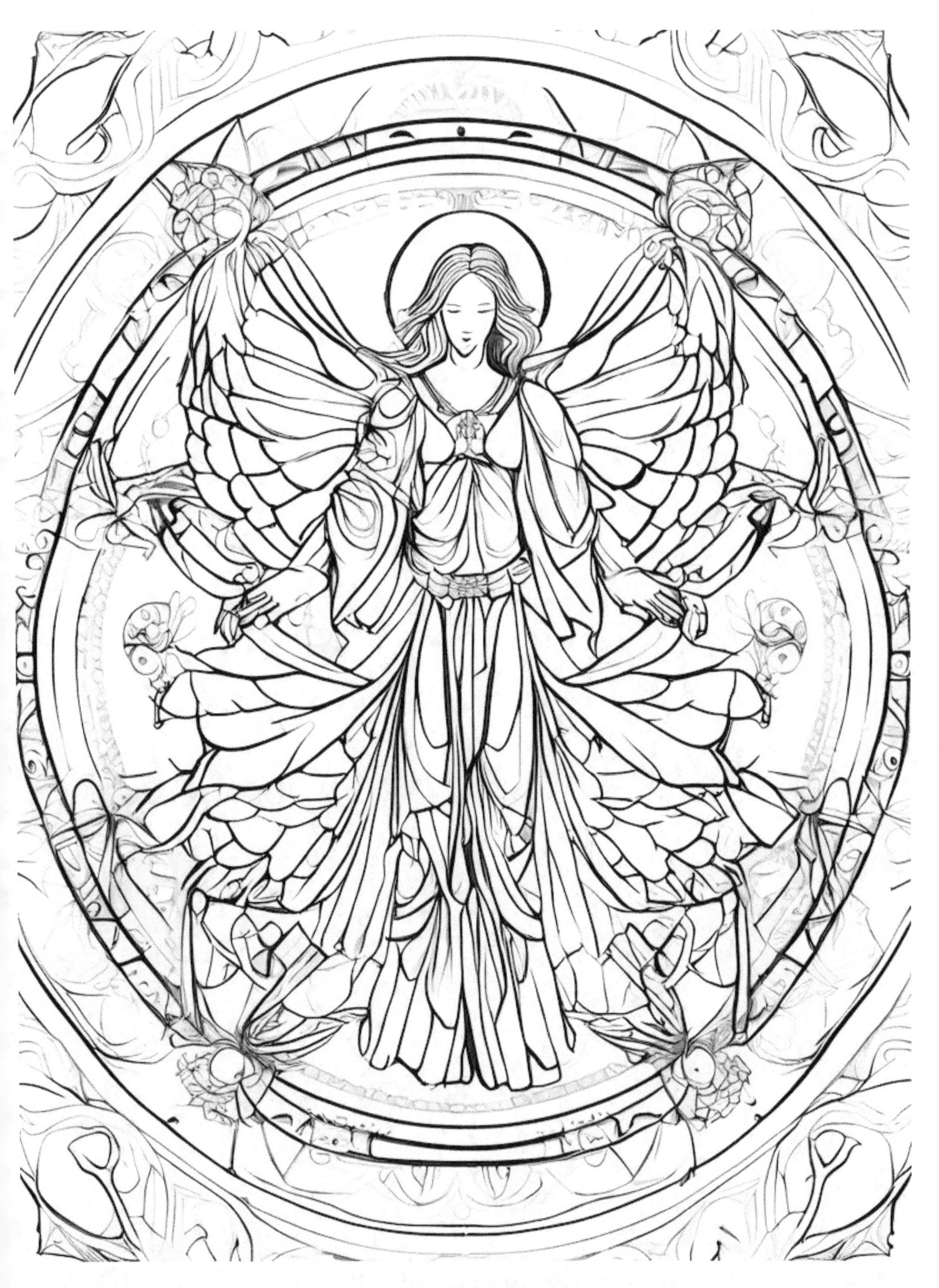

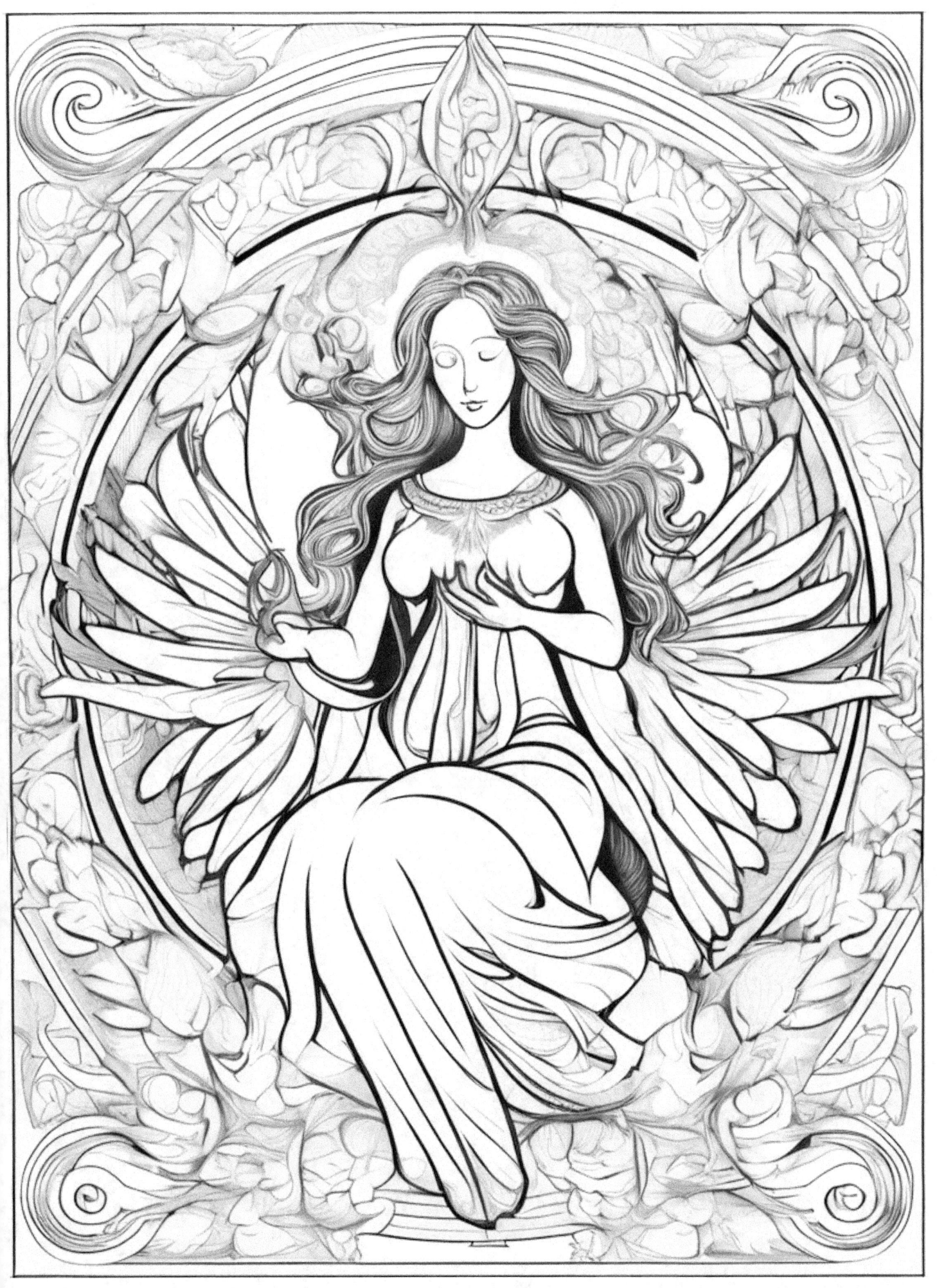

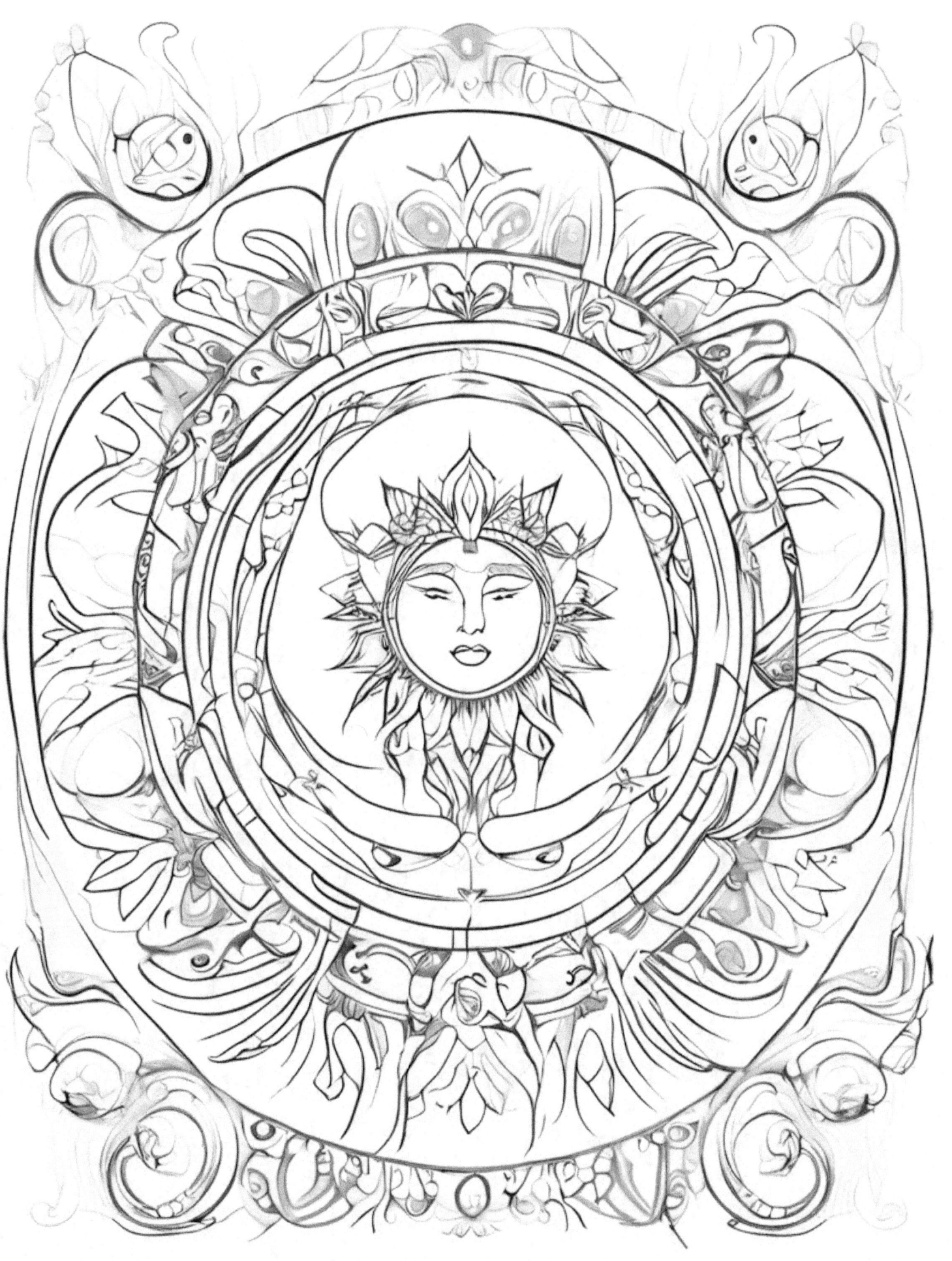

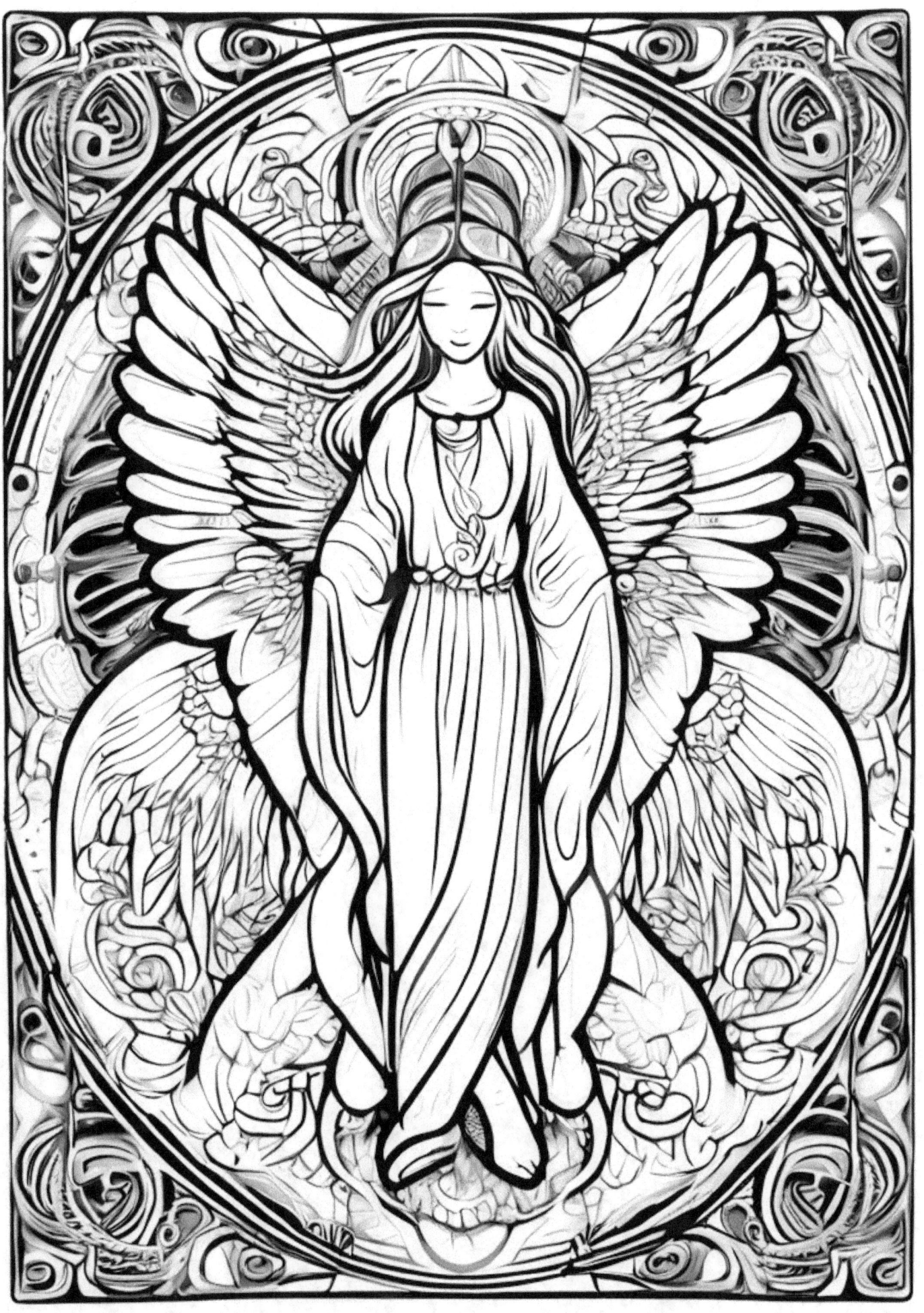

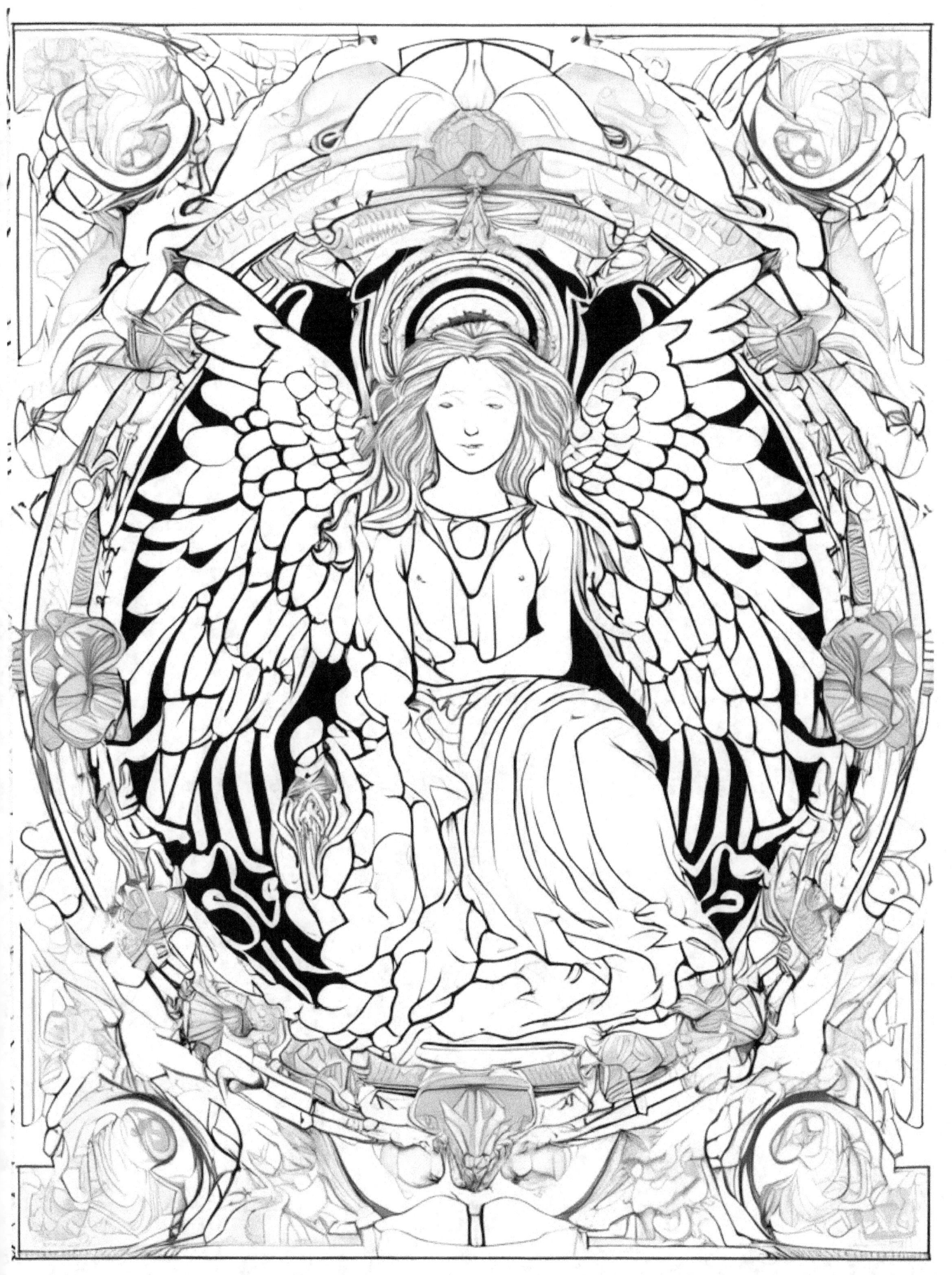

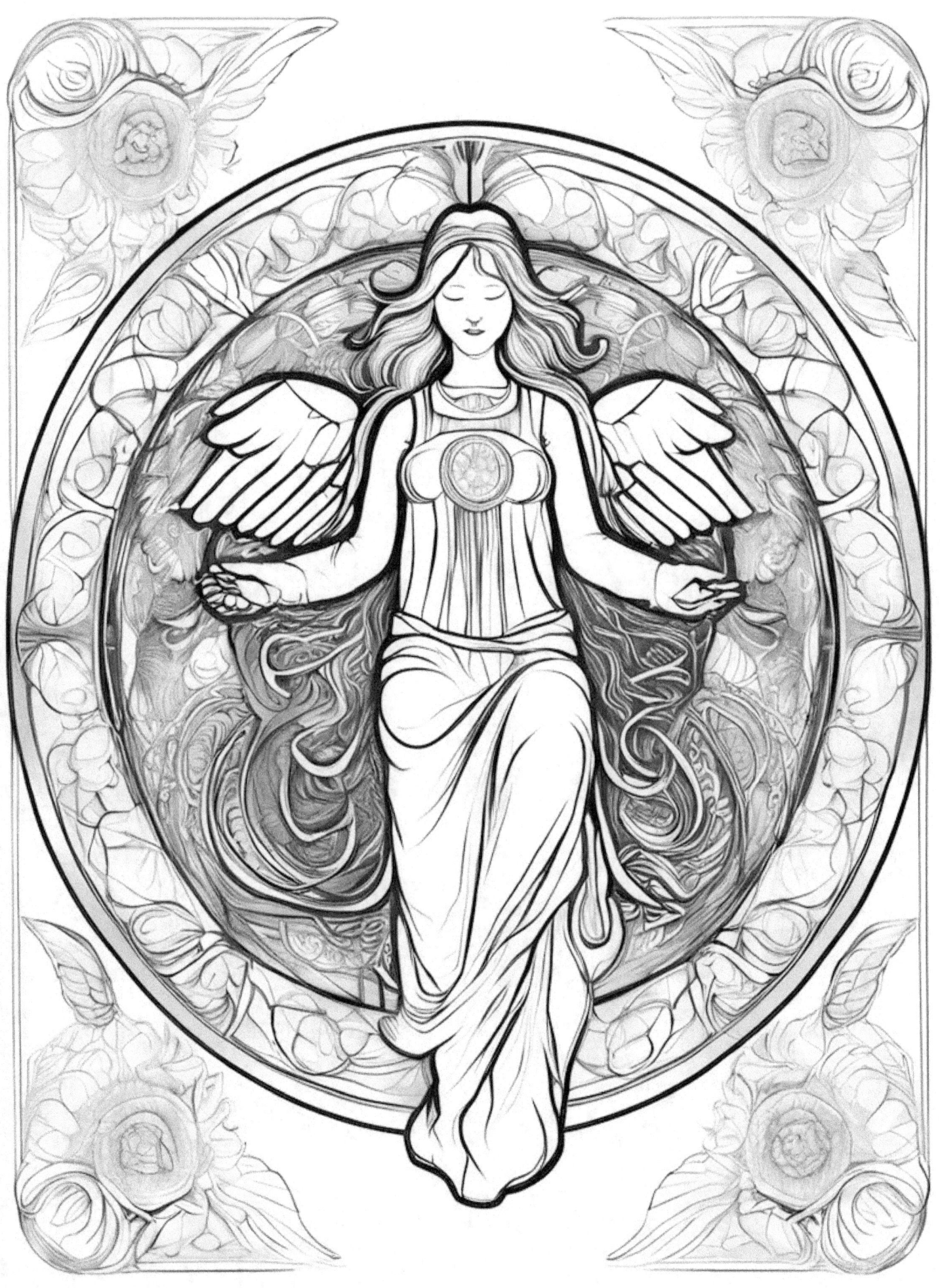

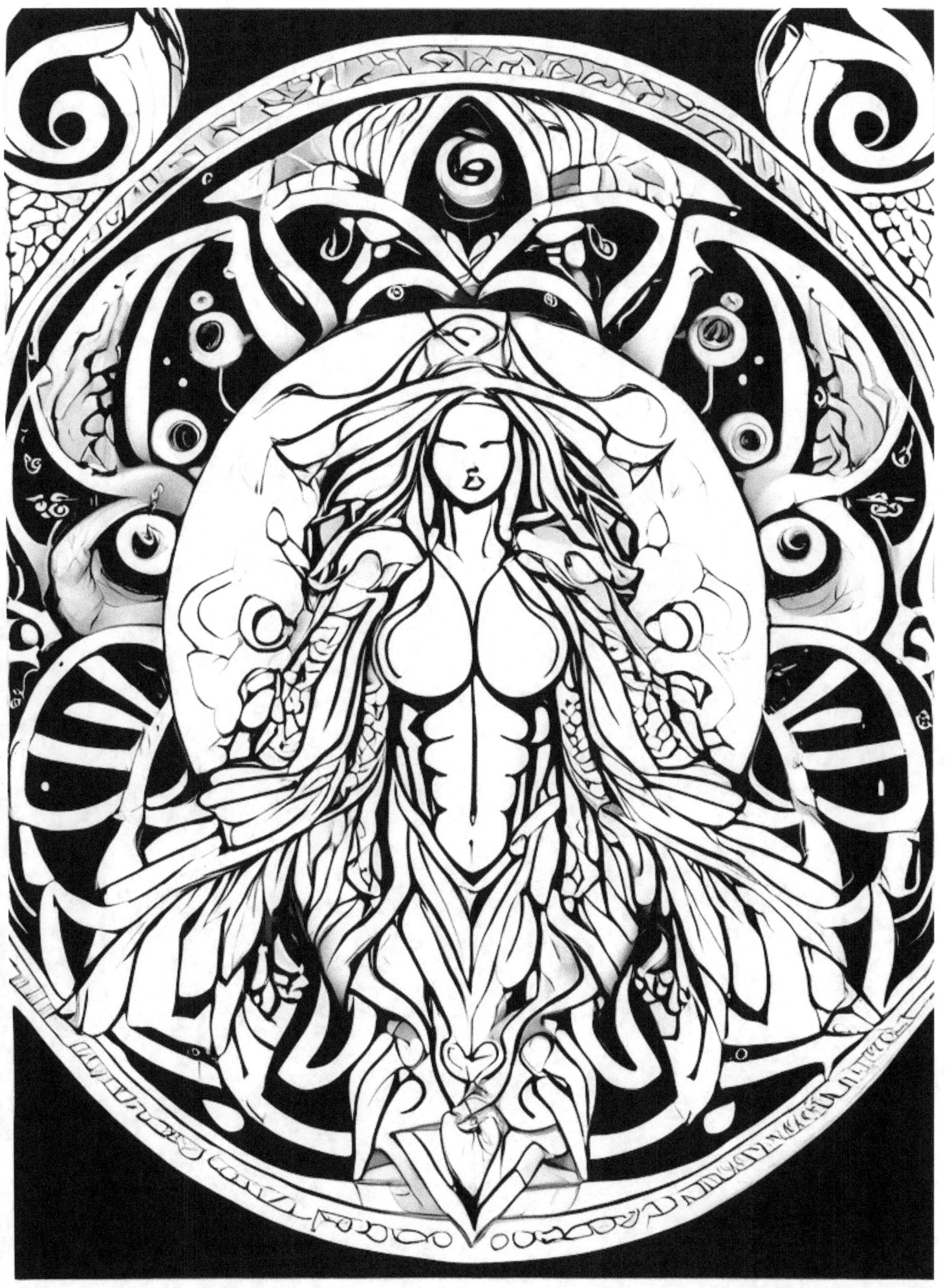

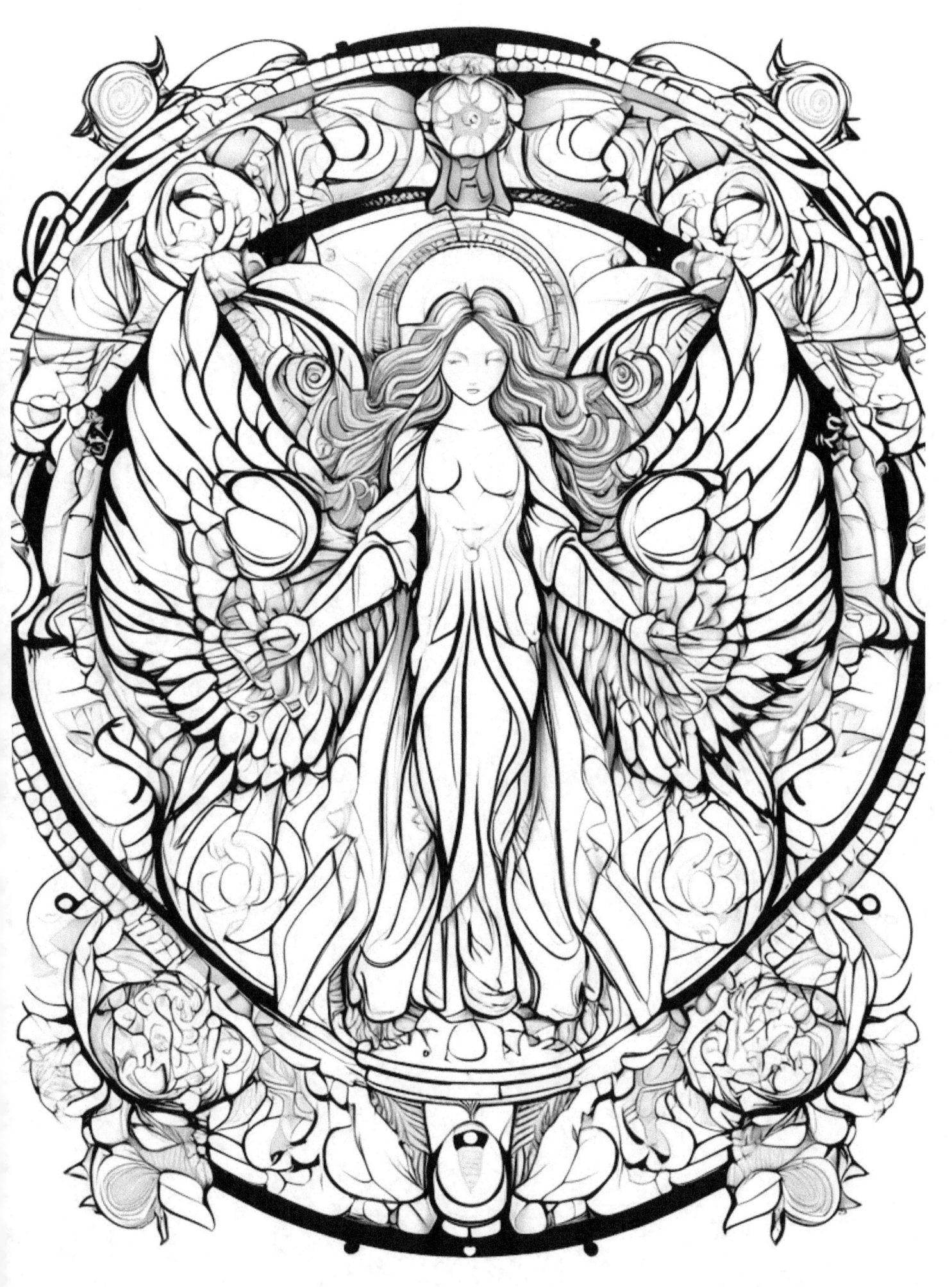

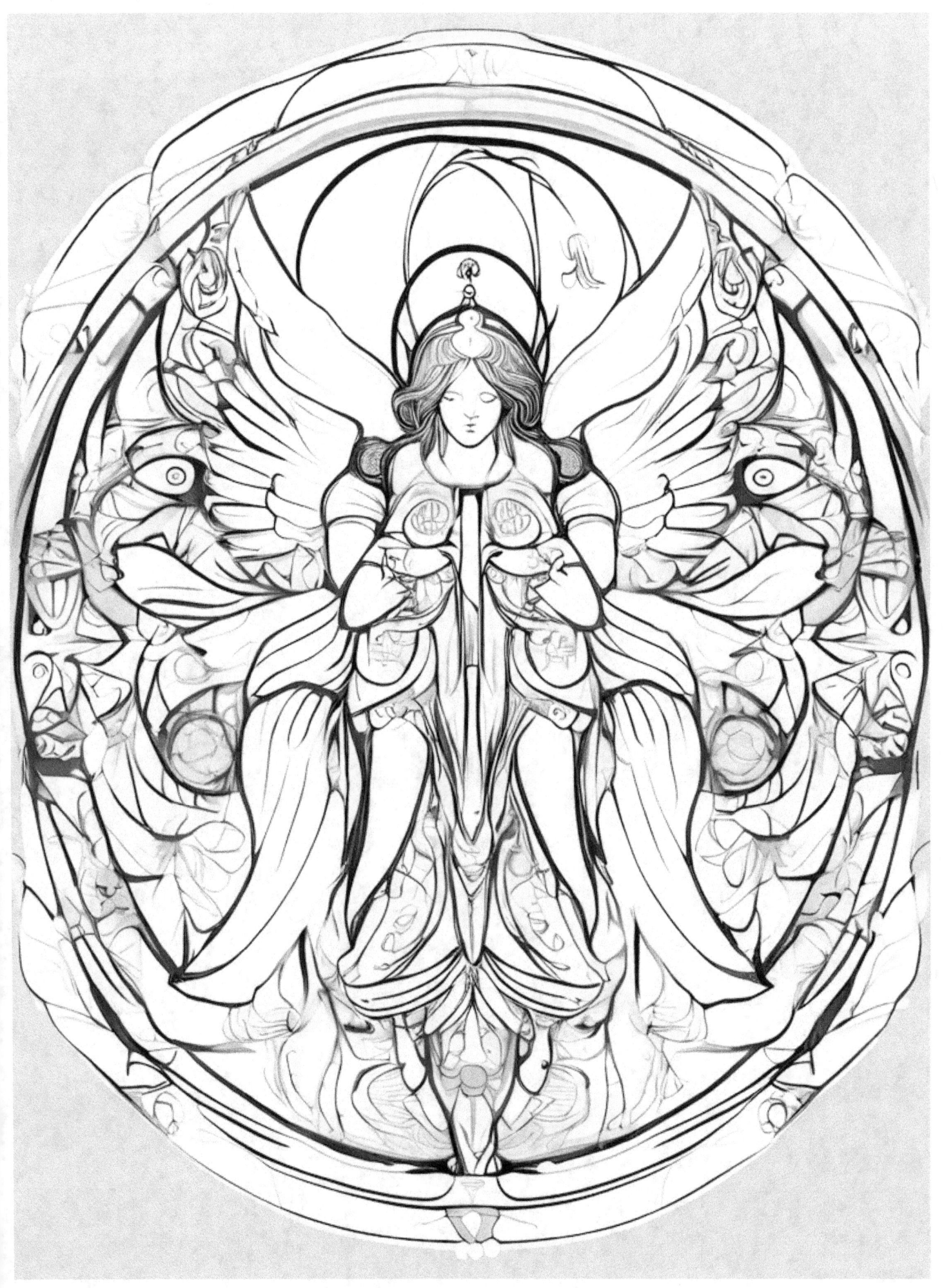

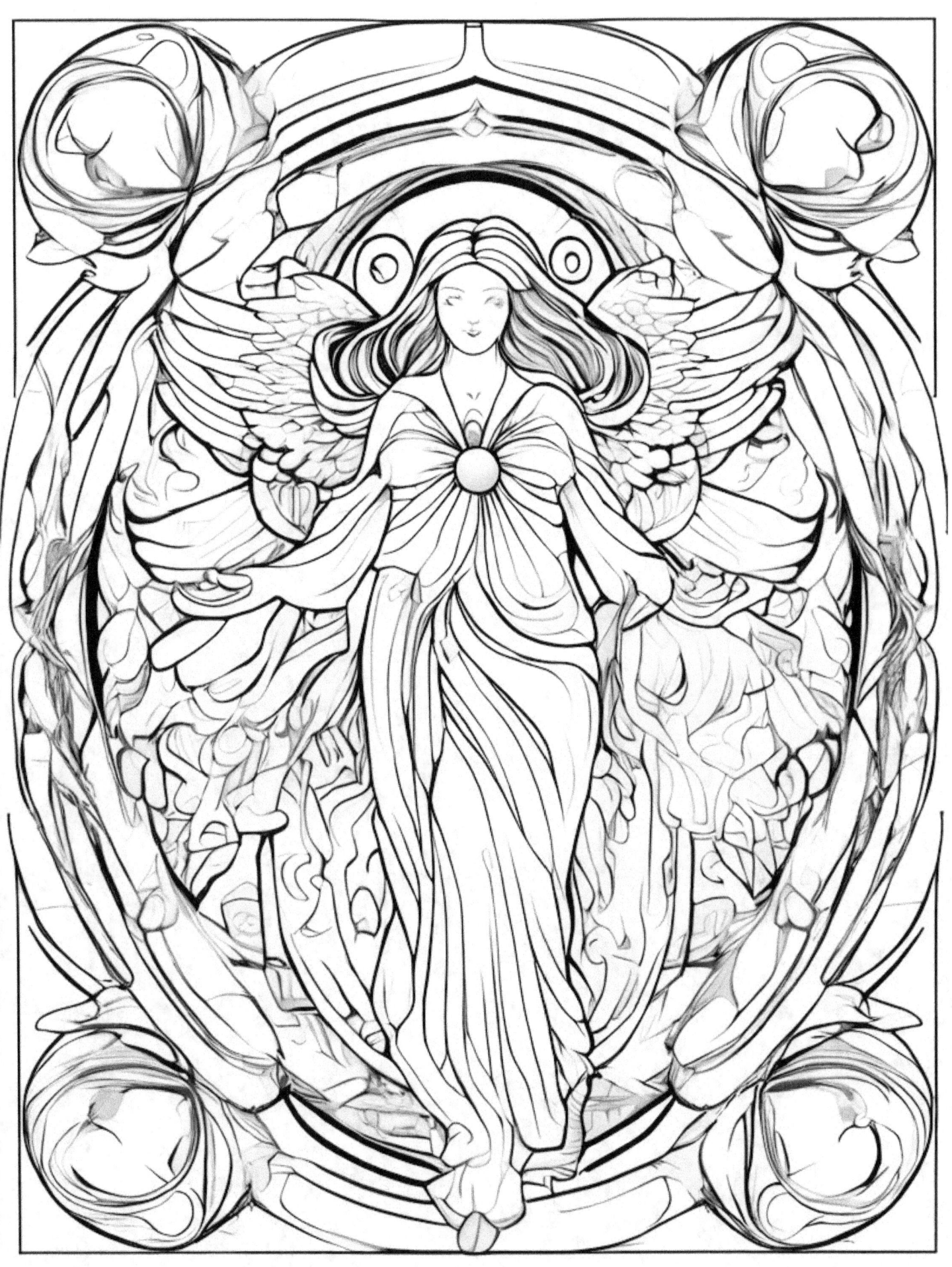

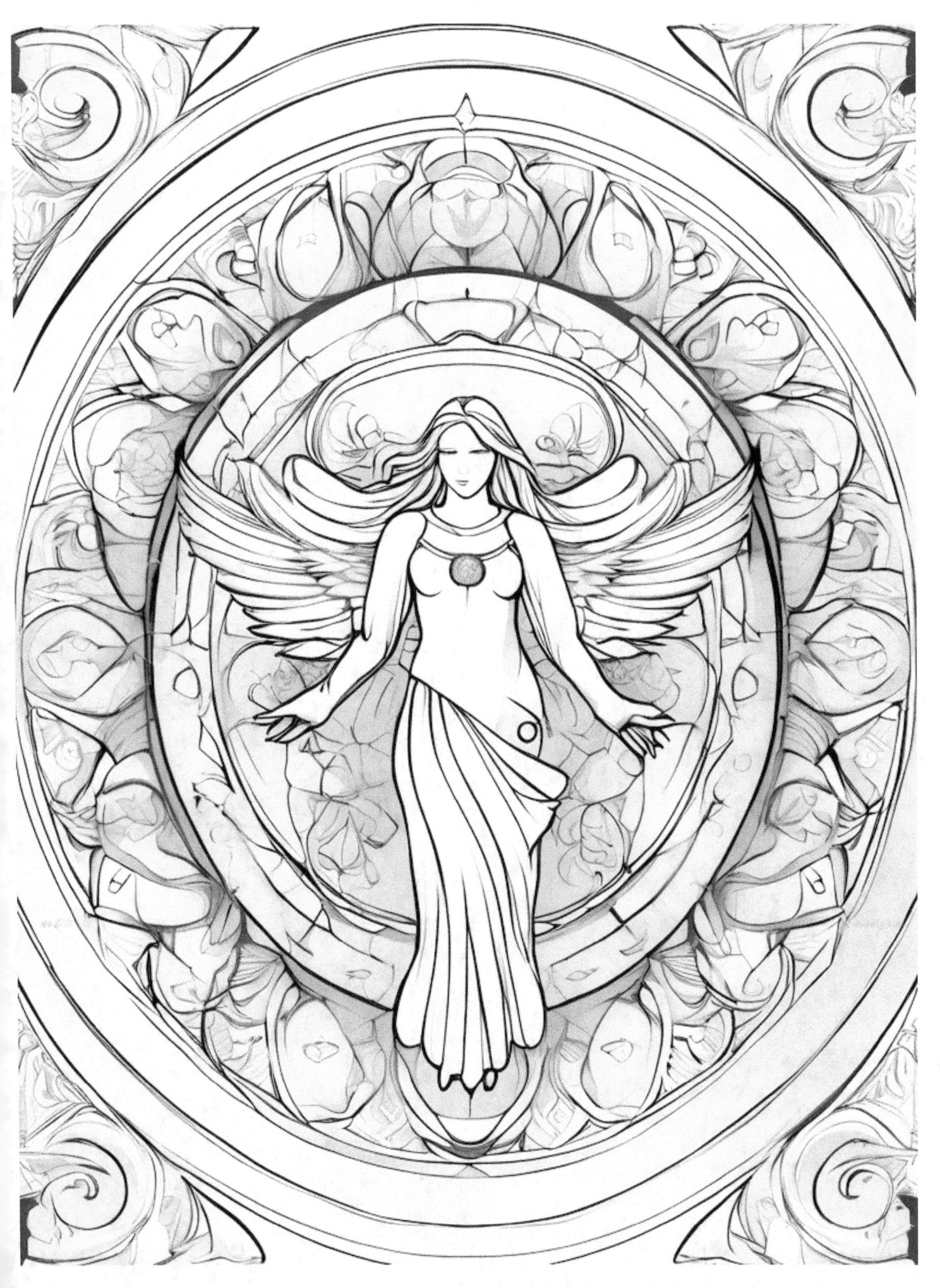

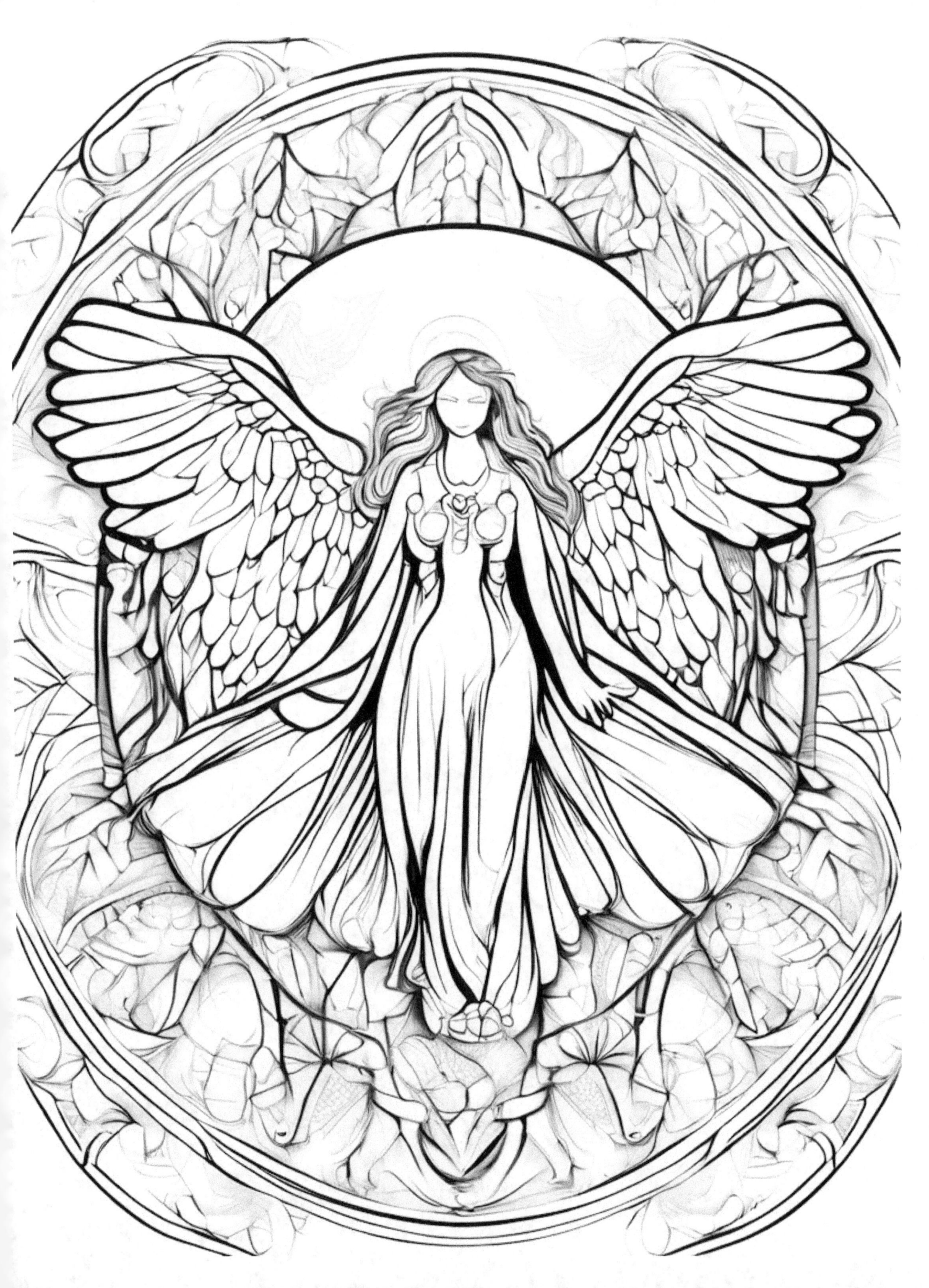

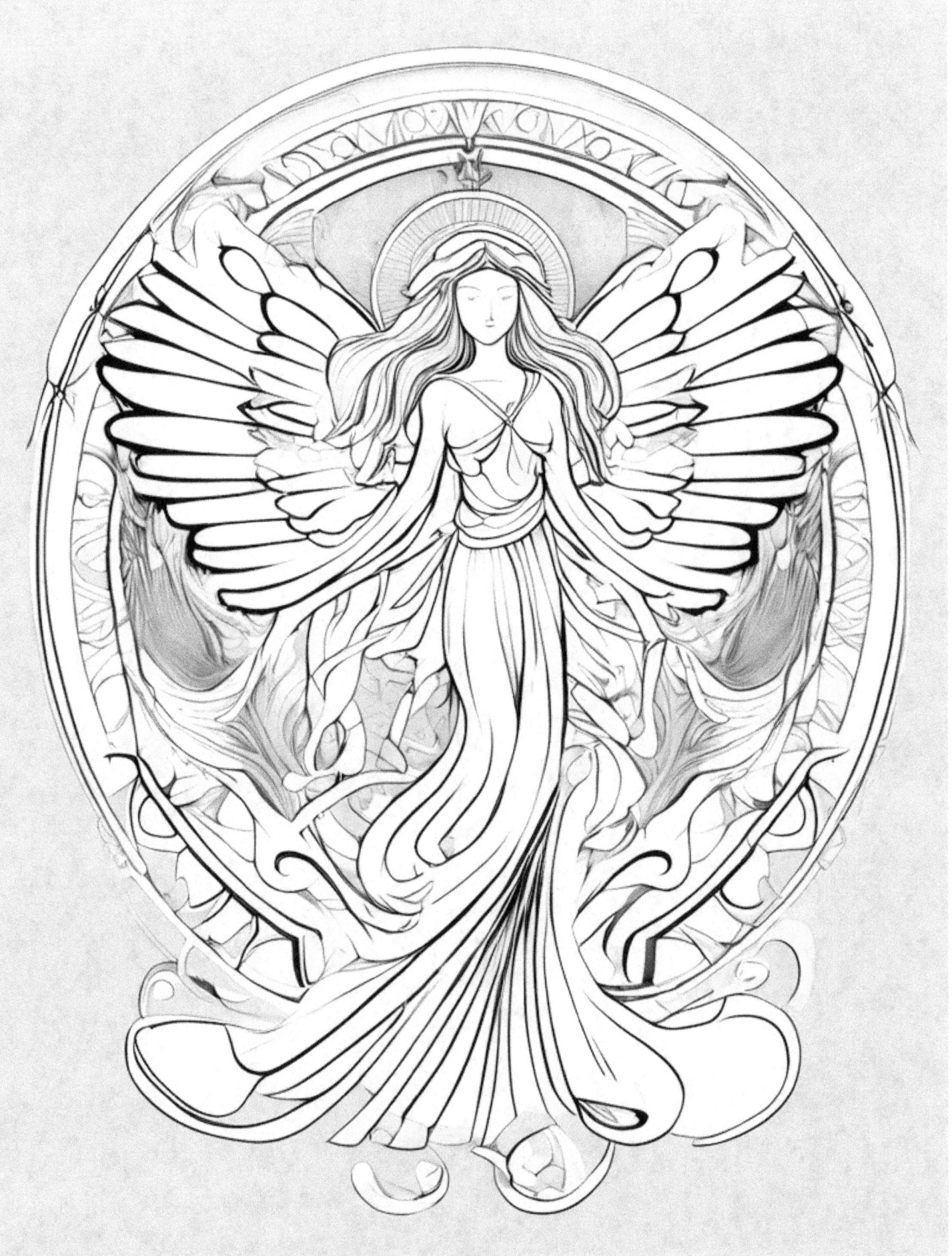

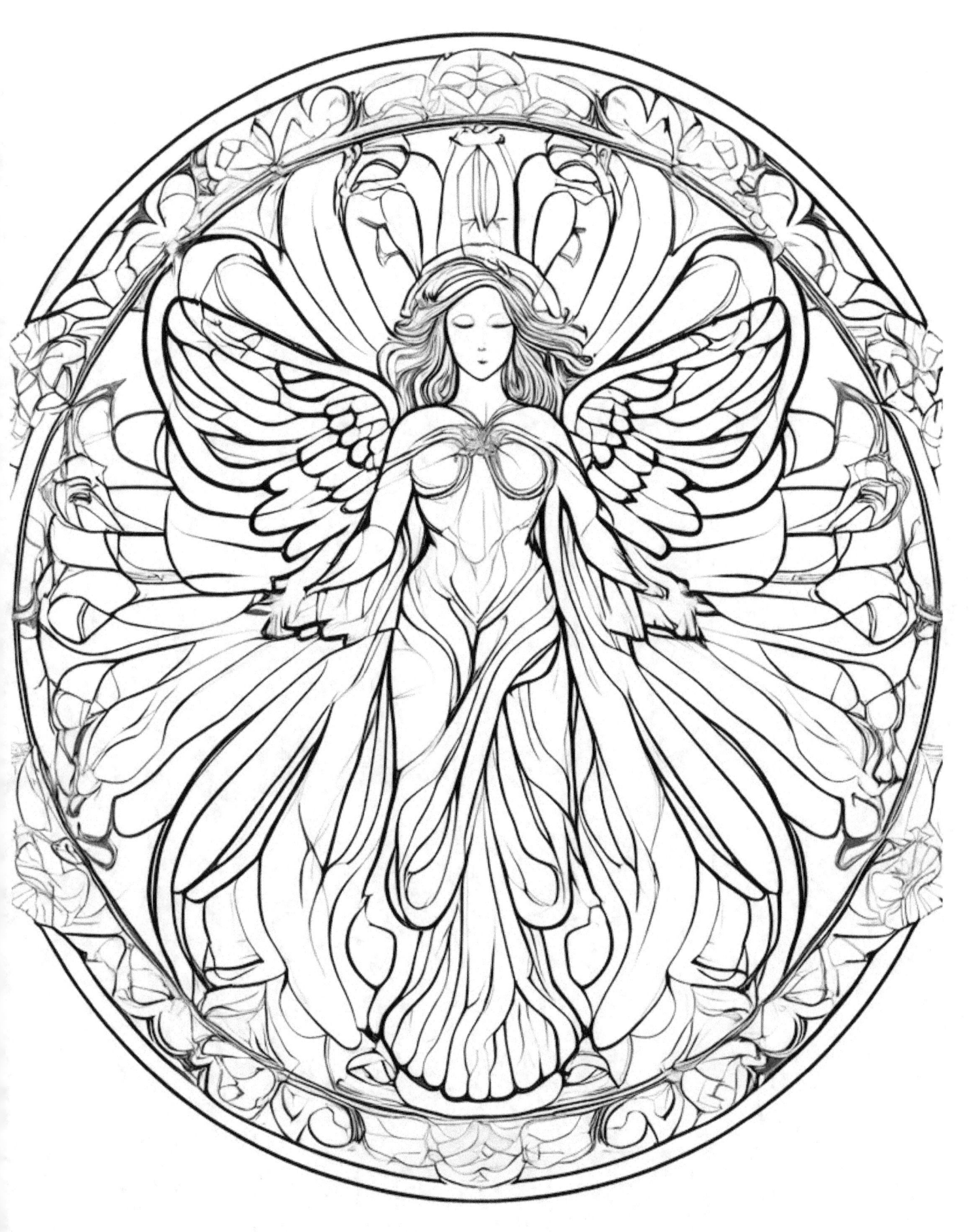

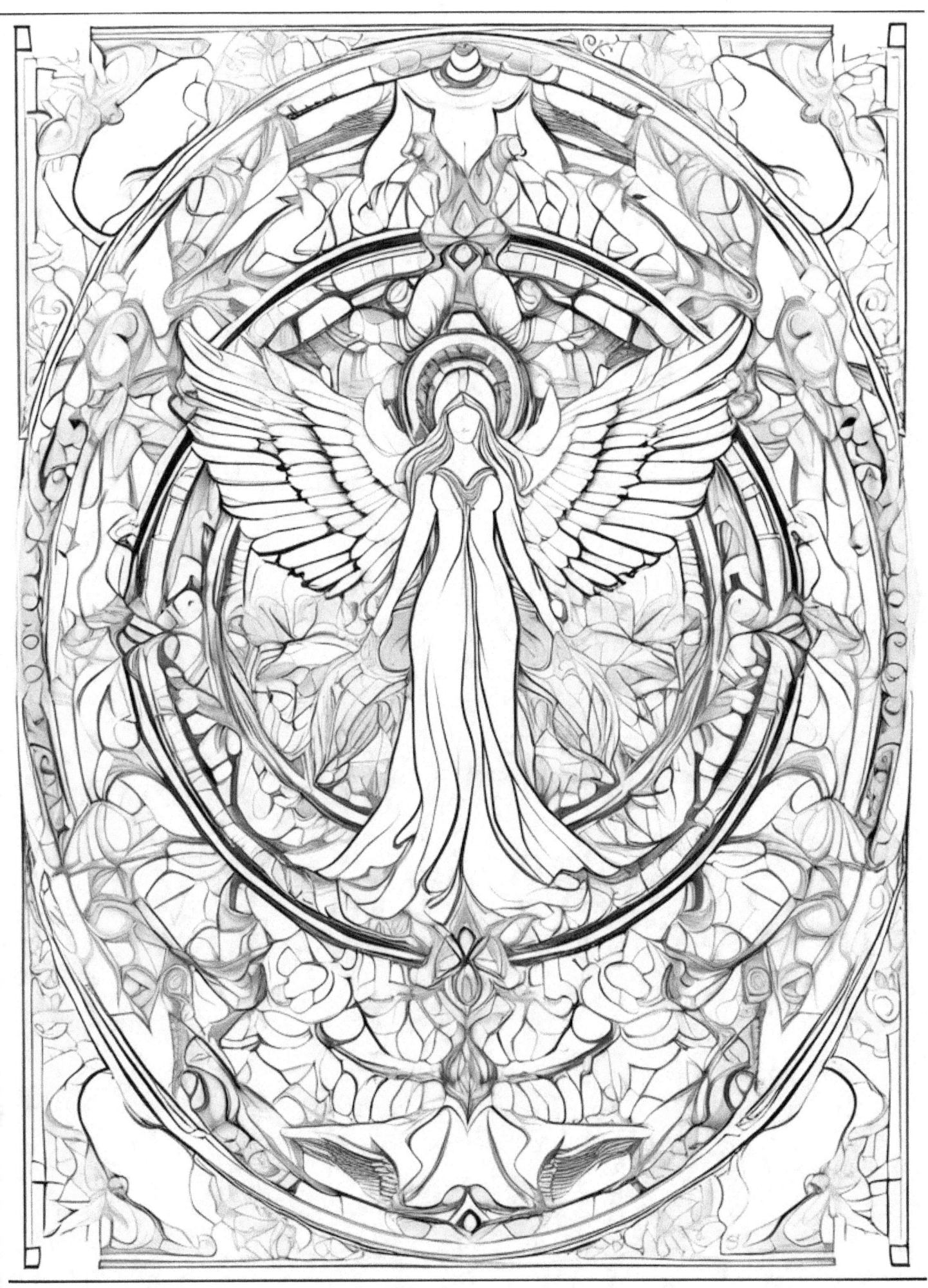

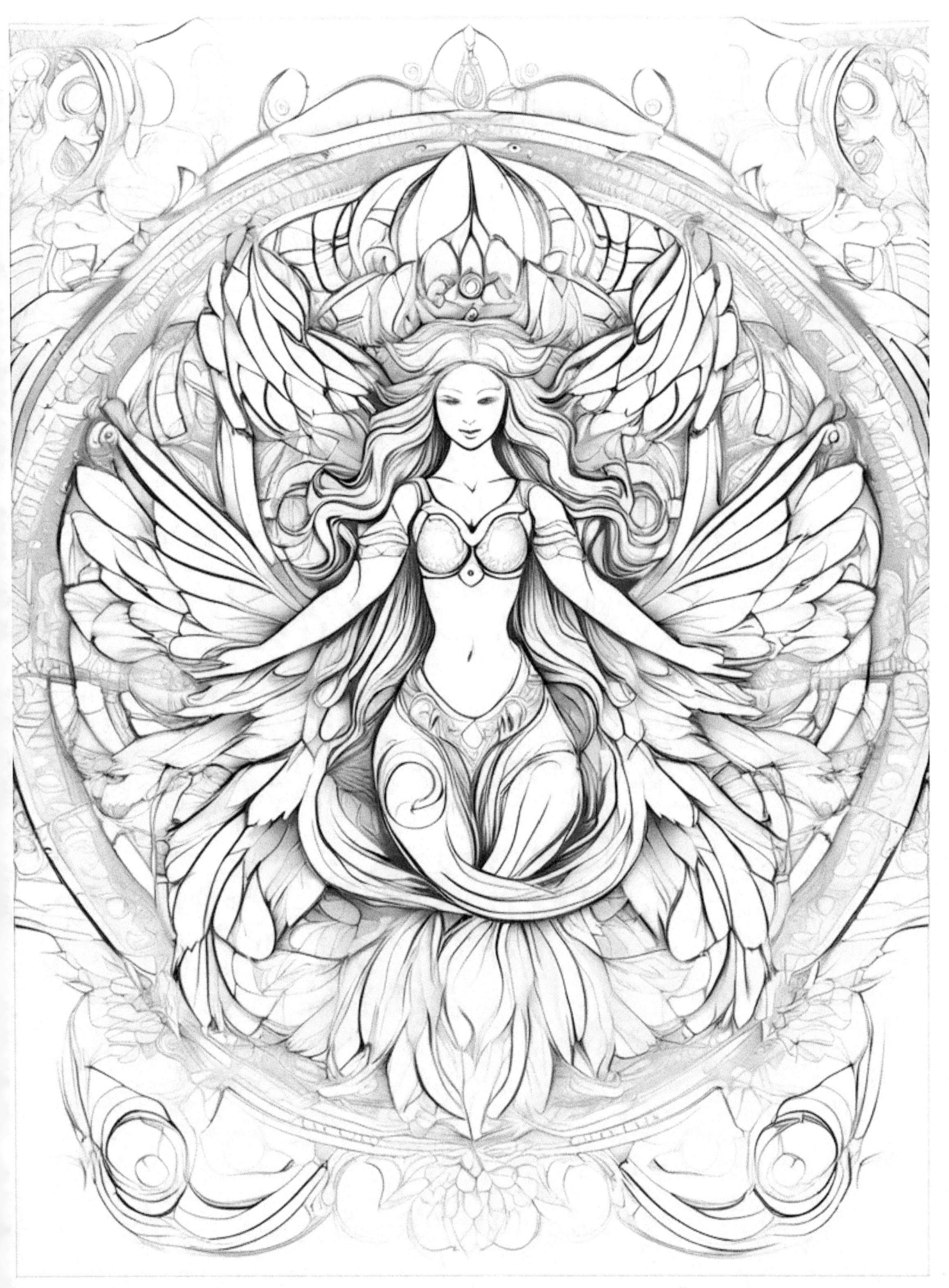

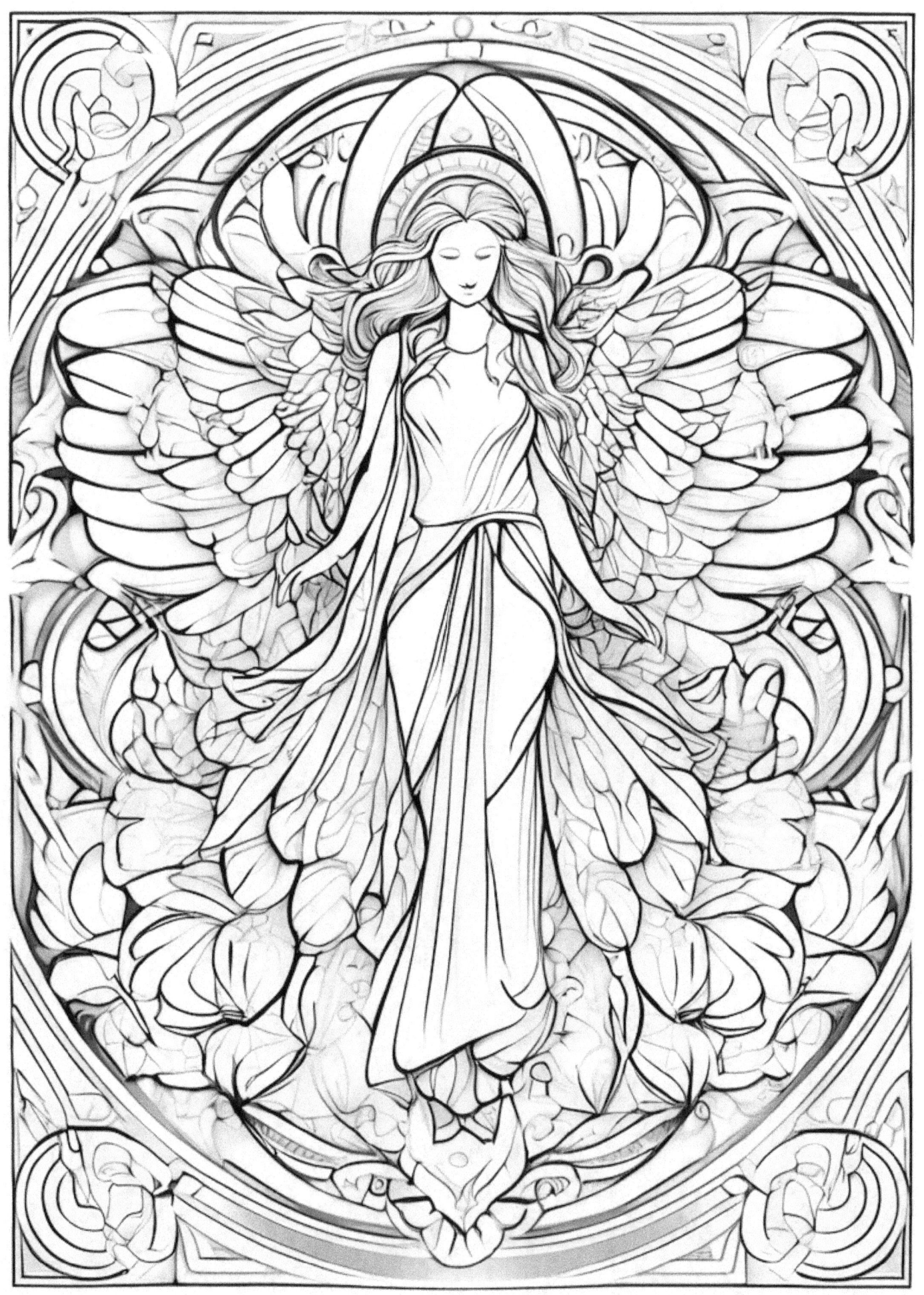

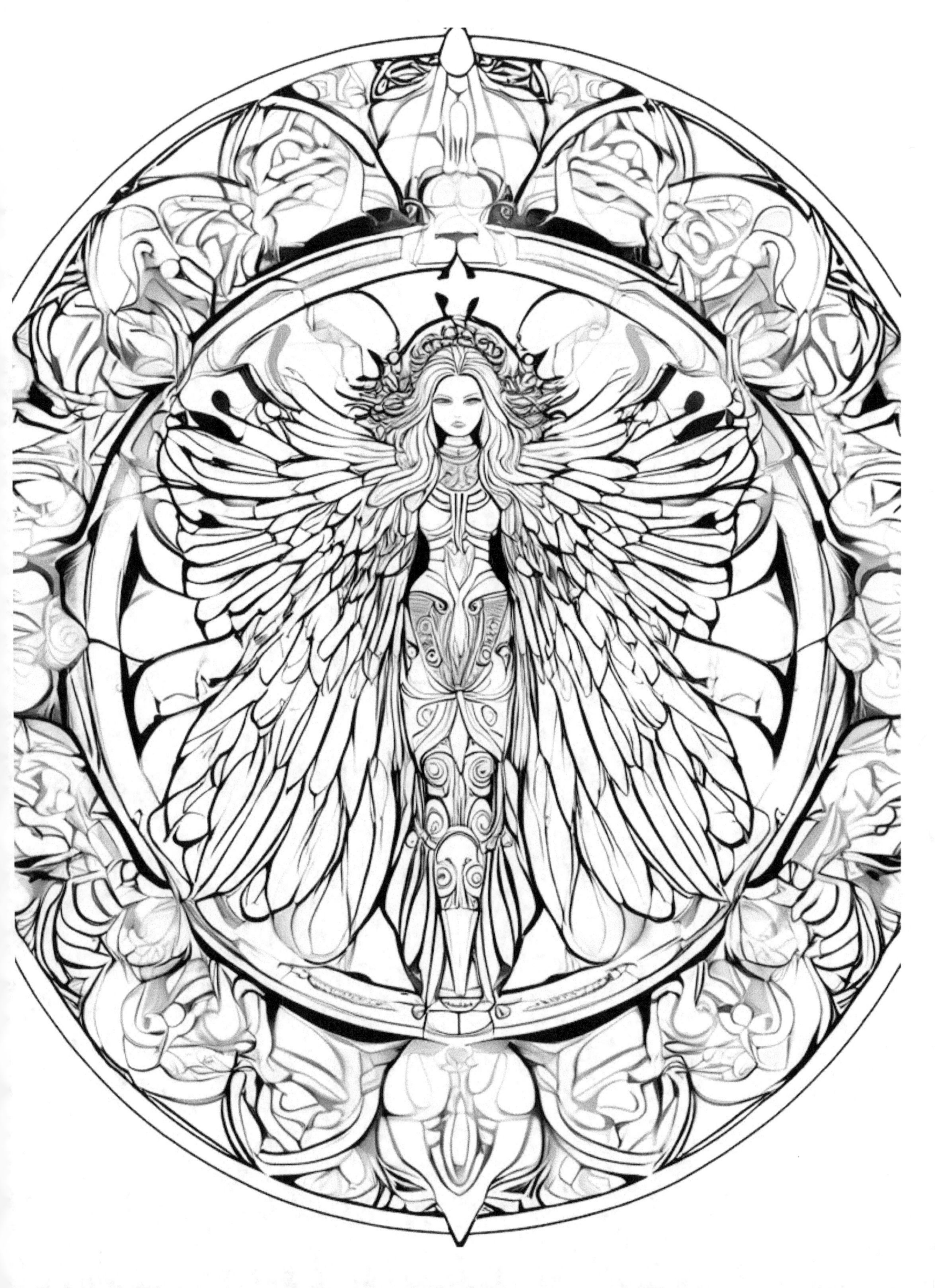

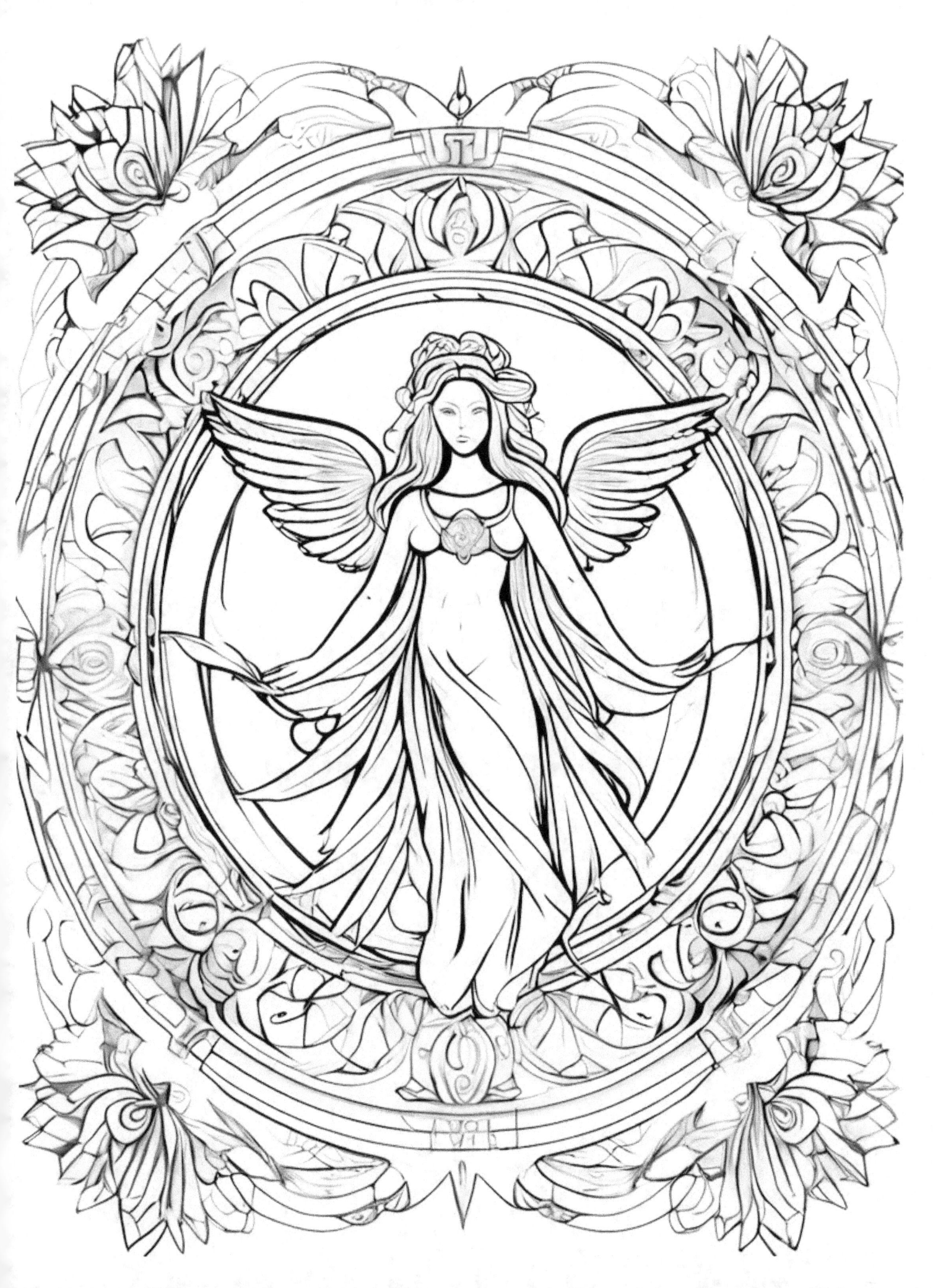

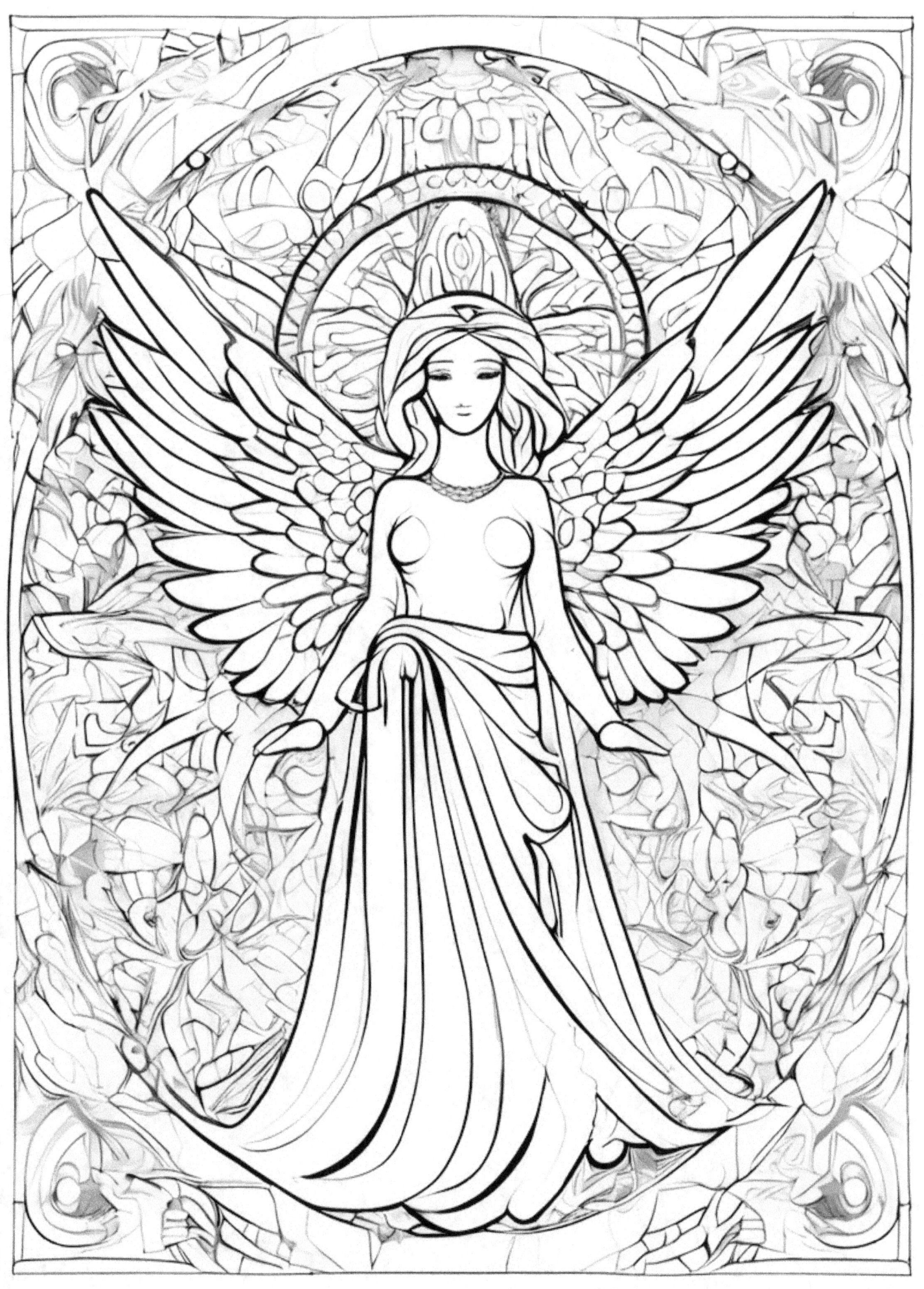

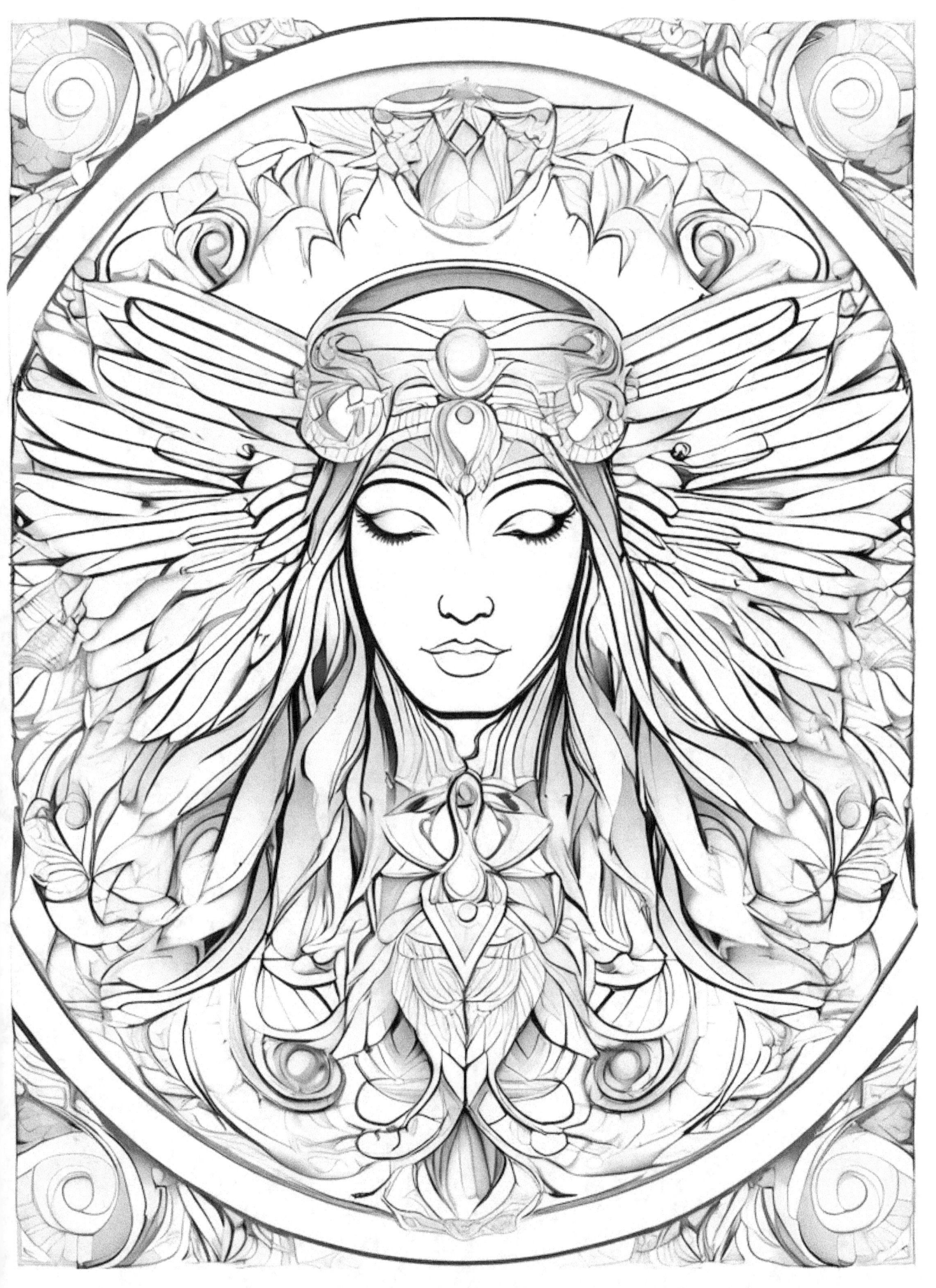

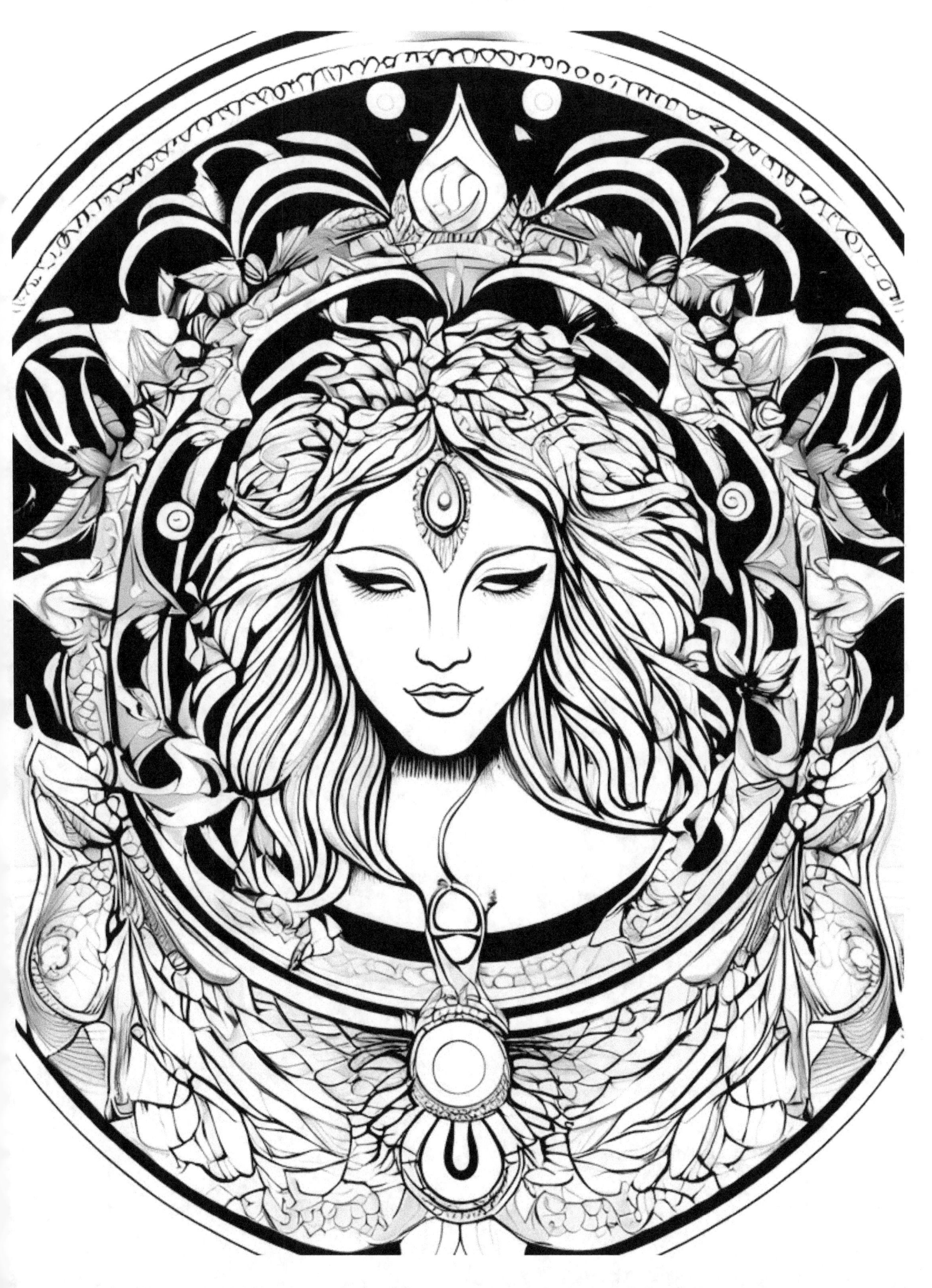

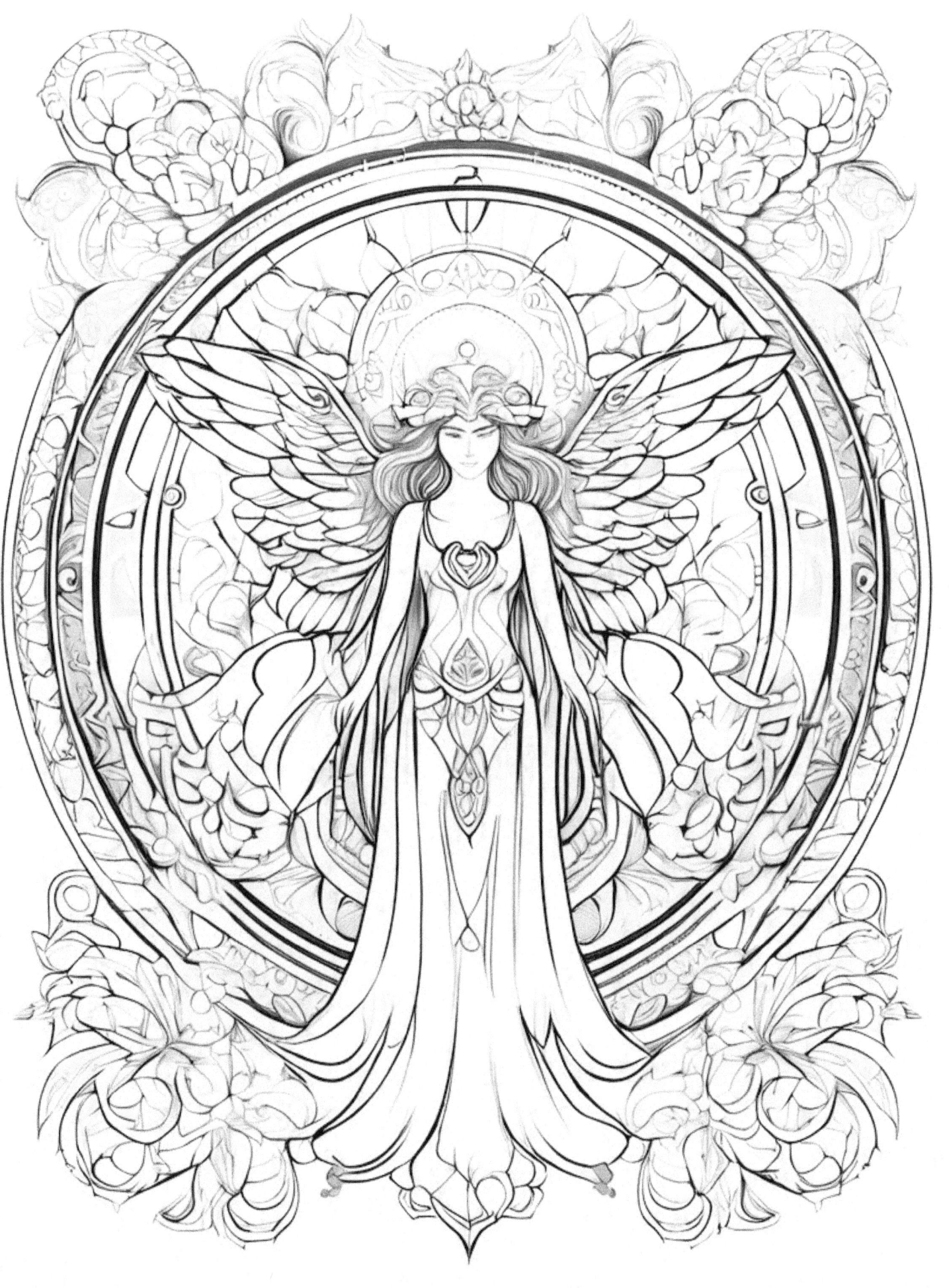

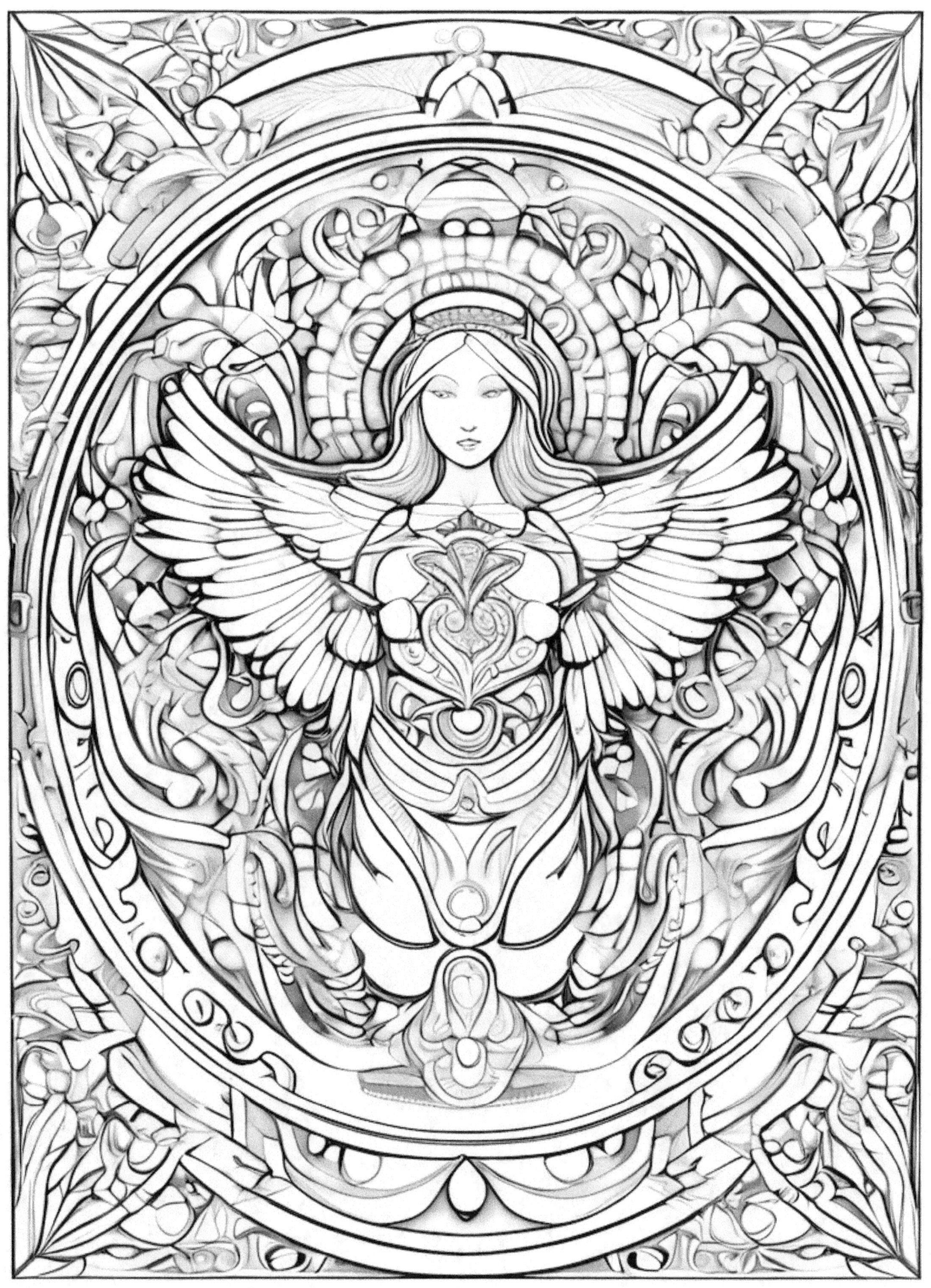

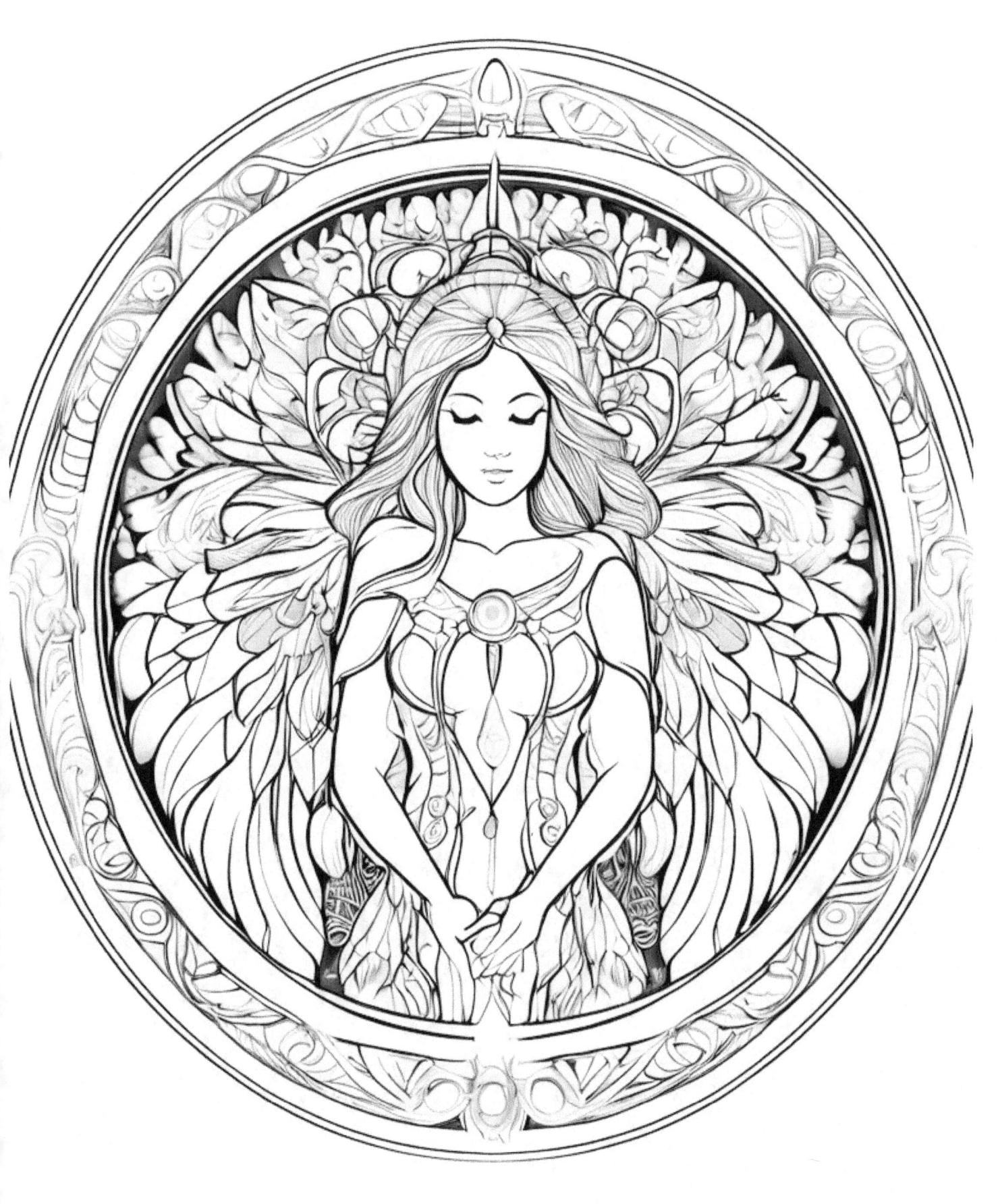

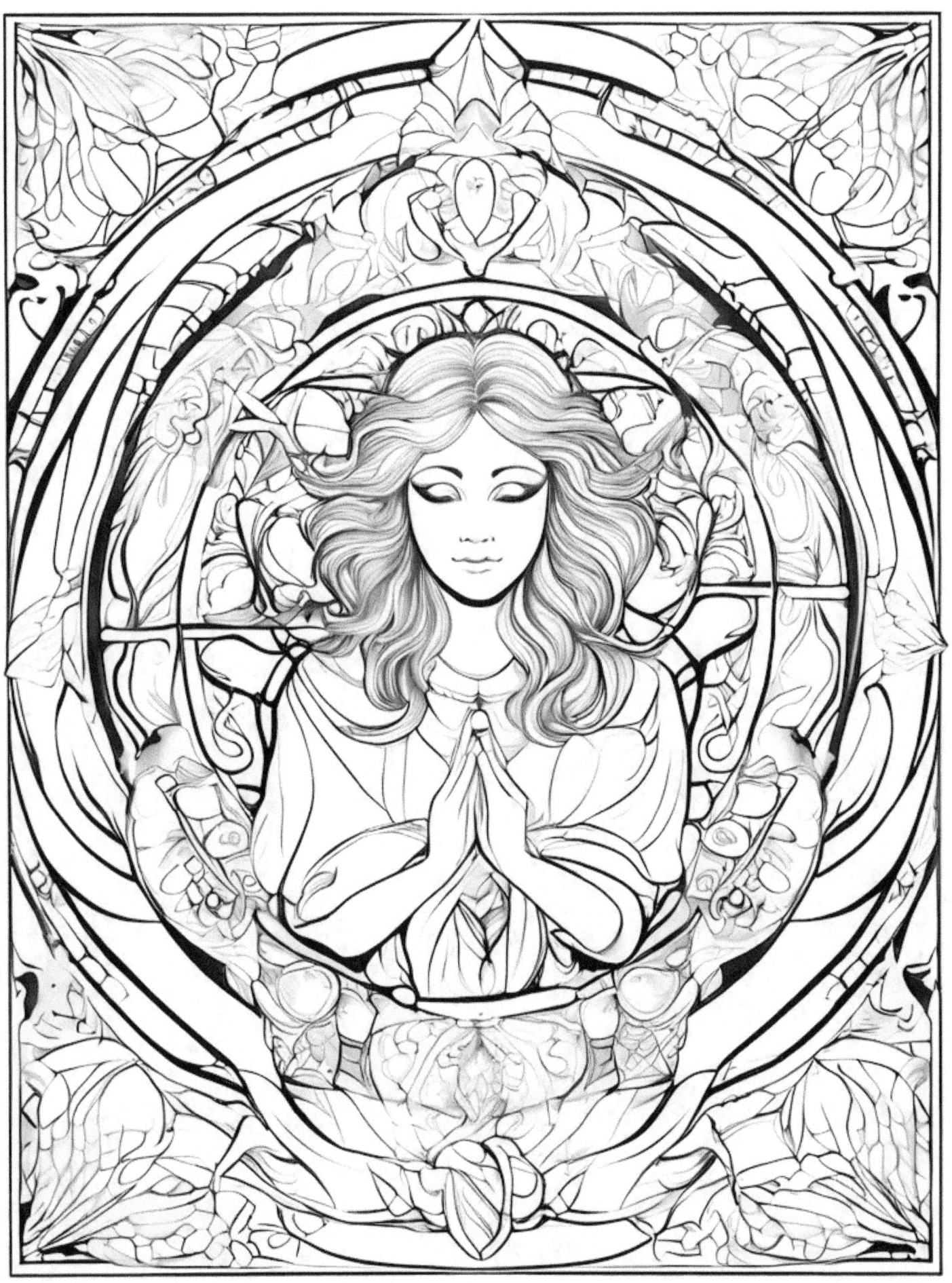

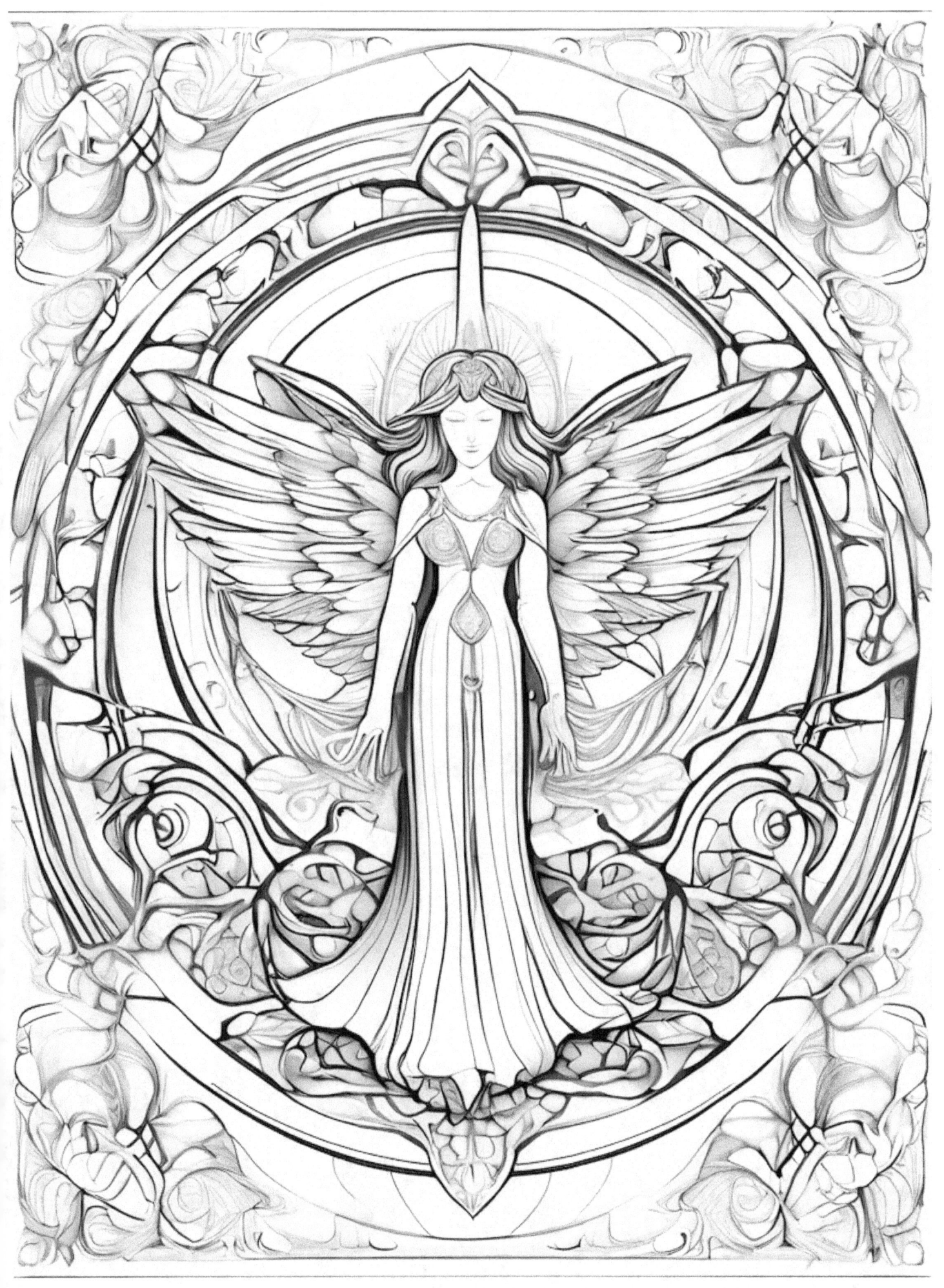

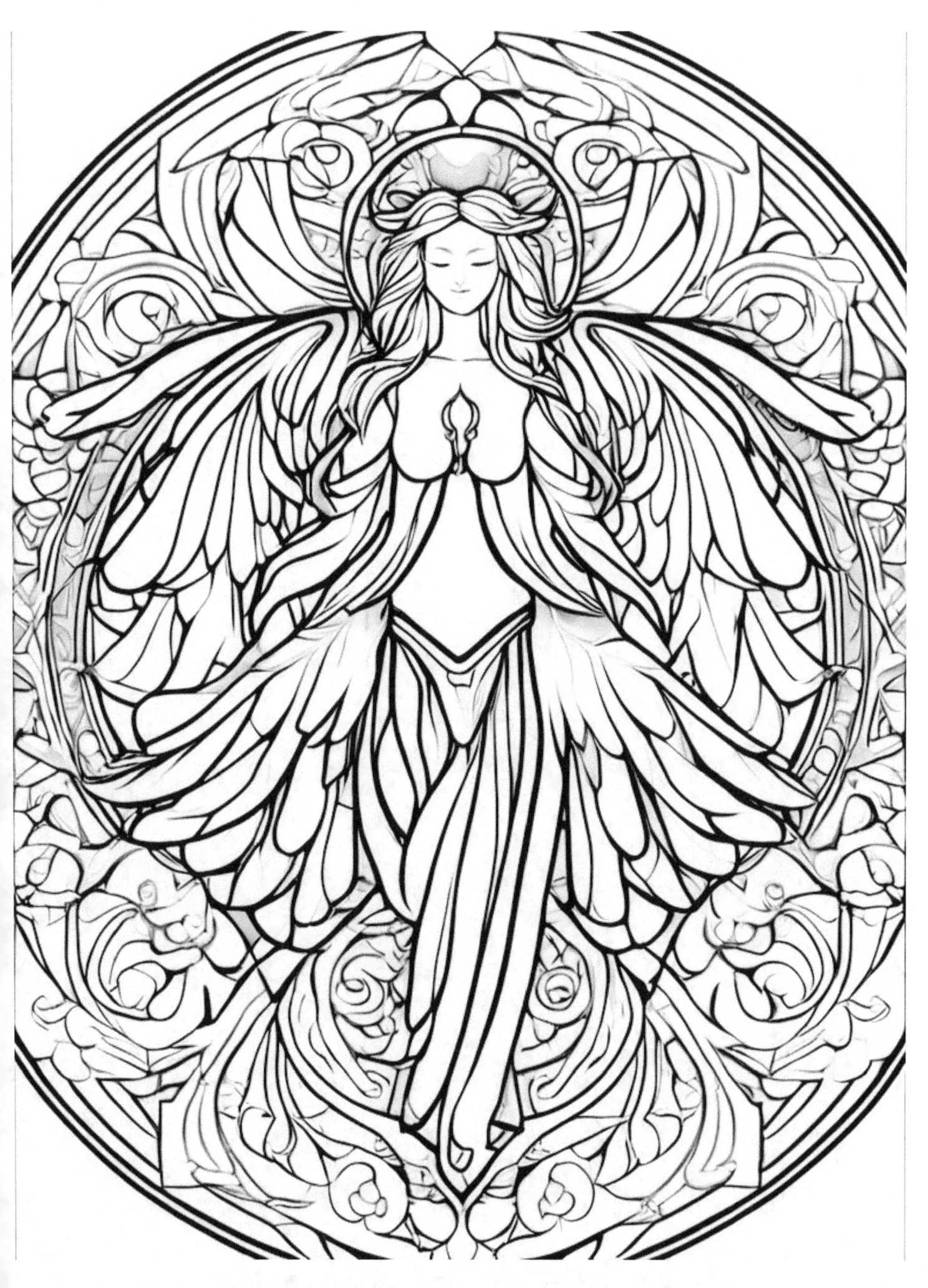

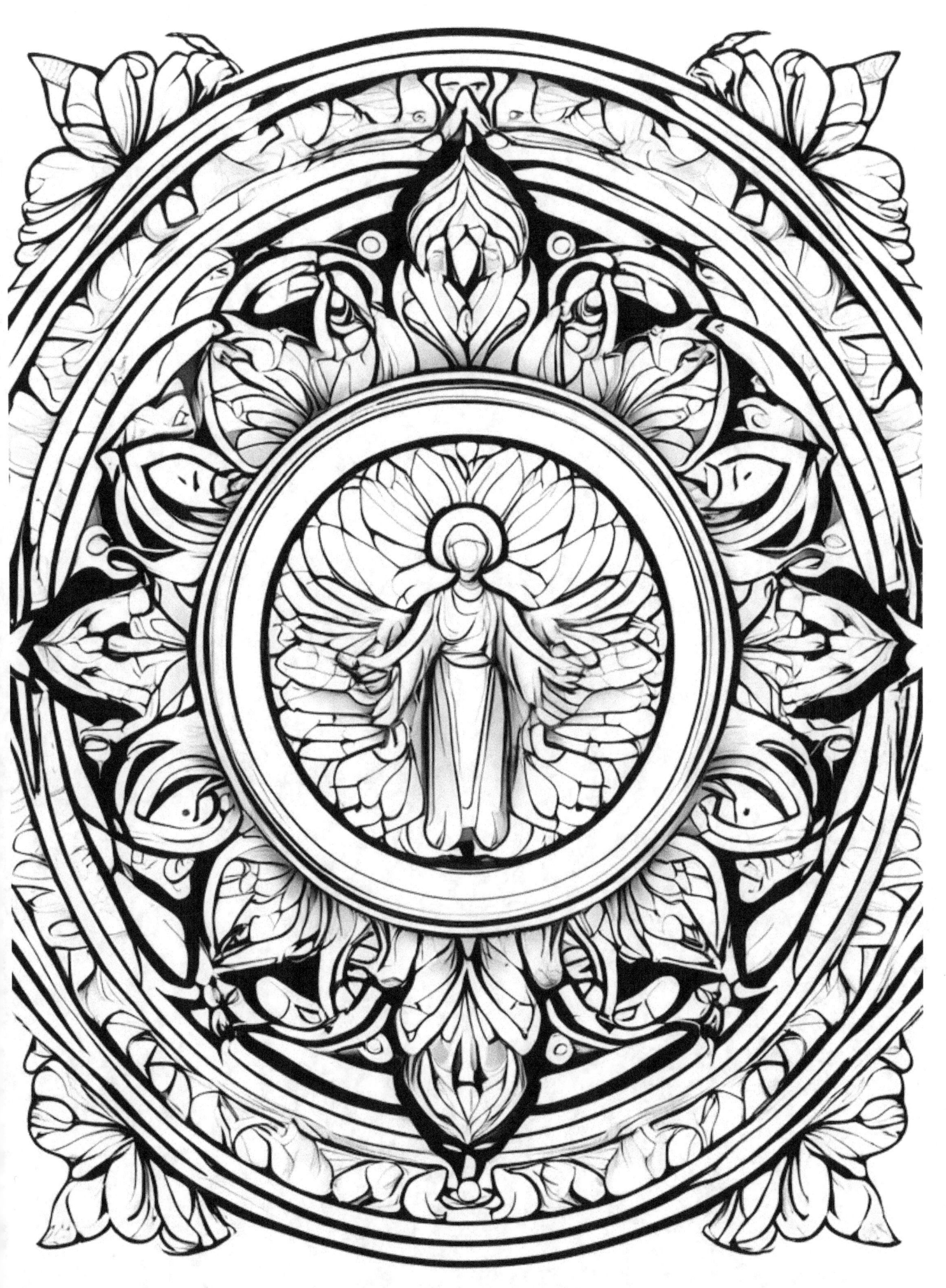

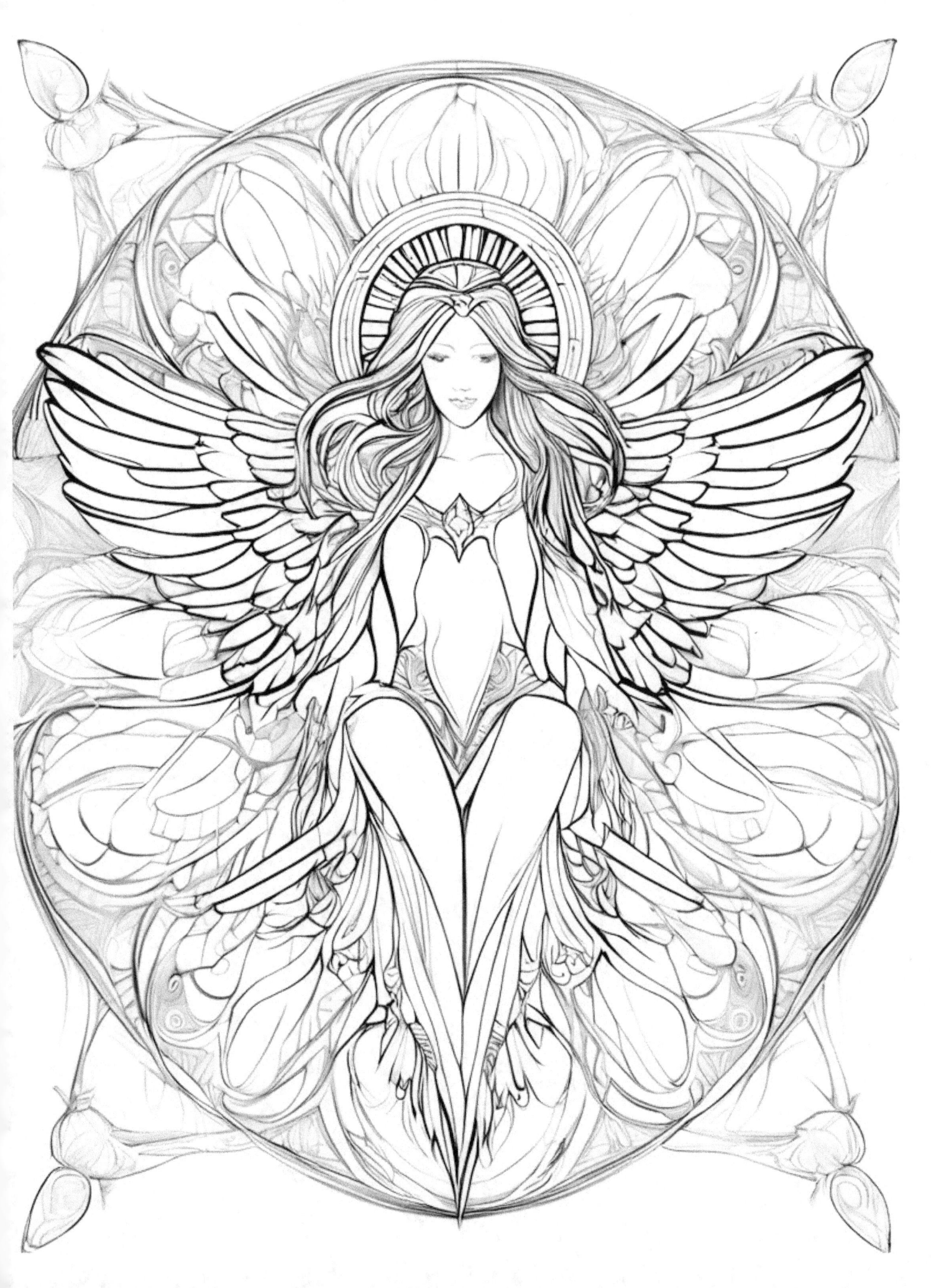

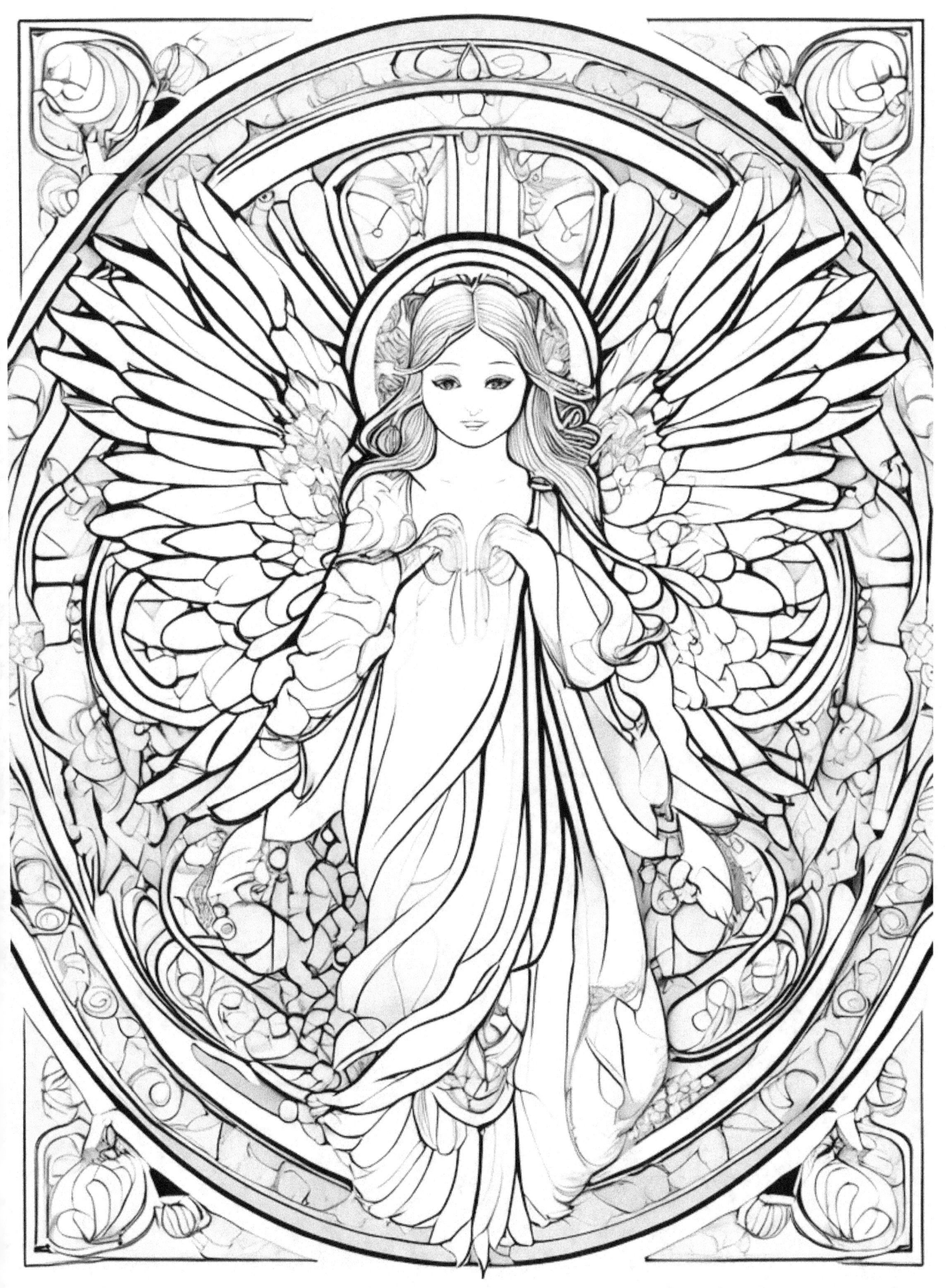

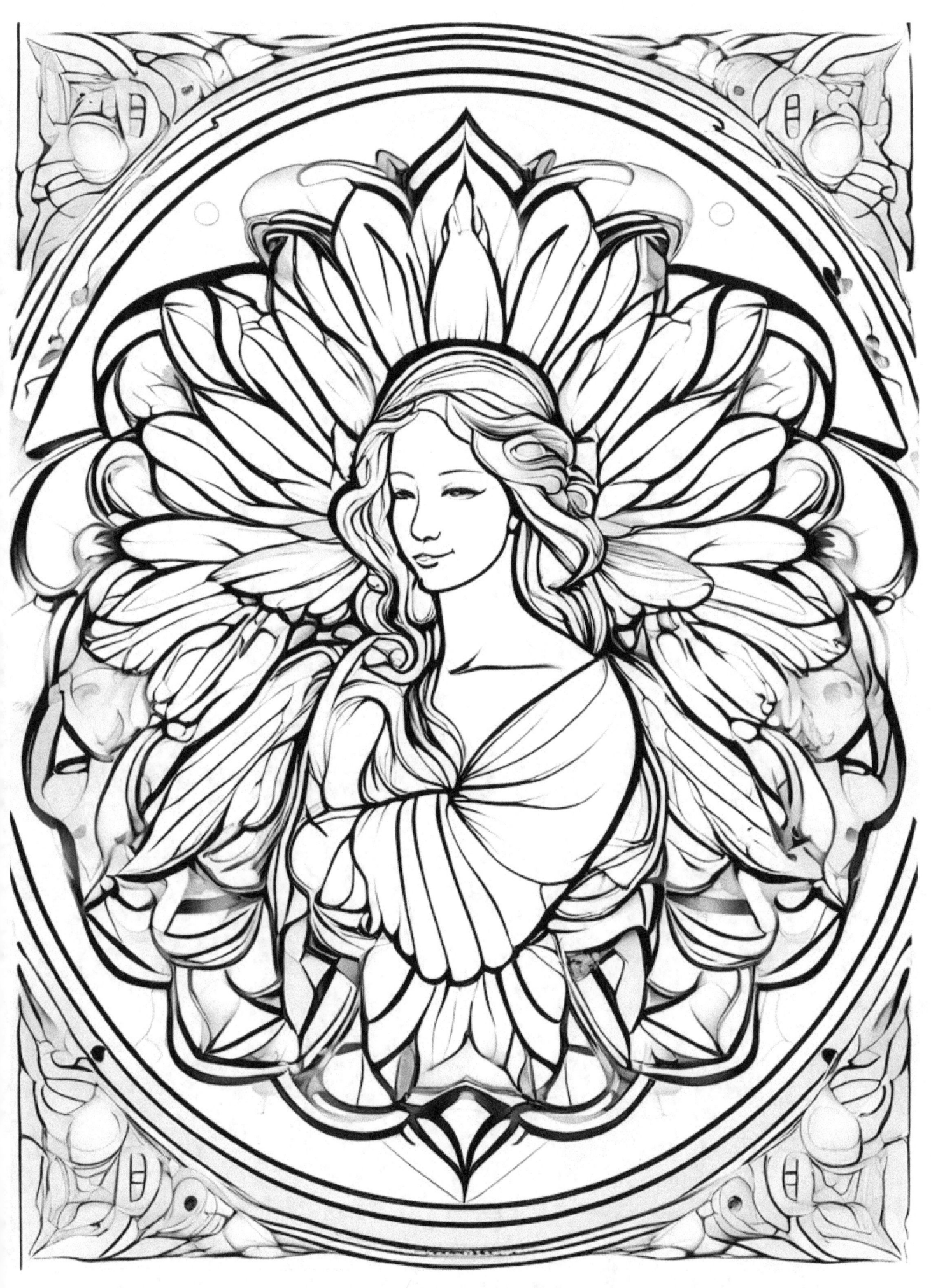

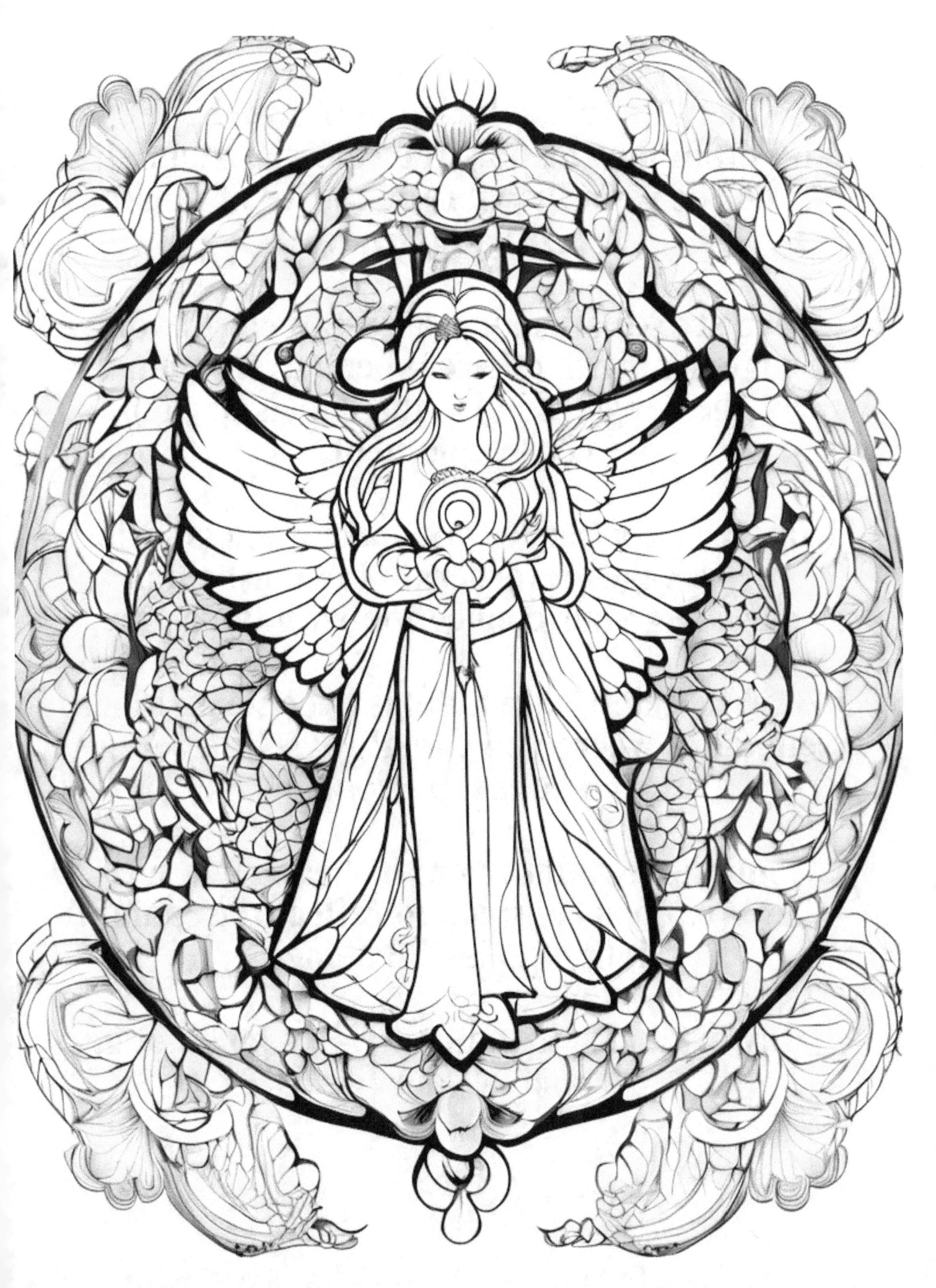

As you close this coloring book, we hope the pages that now display the celestial mandalas also contain the vibrant stories of your spiritual journey.

Each stroke of color is a testament to your engagement with ethereal beauty, a reminder of the wings you give the angels in each chosen pigment.

May the experiences you have when coloring these pages reverberate in your being, nourishing your connection with the divine.

May the celestial mandalas become an inner sanctuary where you can always seek refuge and inspiration.

Continue to paint from the heart, and may your creations continue to reflect the radiant light of celestial beings.

May art and spirituality always go hand in hand in your life.

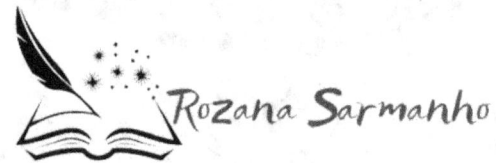

Rozana Sarmanho

www.ingramcontent.com/pod-product-compliance
Lightning Source LLC
Chambersburg PA
CBHW080955290526

45795CB00009B/2961